THIS BOOK

BELONGS TO

....

....

Thank you for Purchasing my book and taking the time to read it from front to back. I am always grateful when a reader chooses my work and I hope you enjoyed it!

With the vast selection available online, I am touched that you chose to be purchasing my work and take valuable time out of your life to read it. My hope is that you feel you made the right decision.

I very much would like to know what you thought of the book. Please take the time to write an honest and informative review on Amazon.com. Your experience and opinions will be of great benefit to me and those readers looking to make an informed choice.

With much thanks.

Table of Contents

Introduction

"You don't stop laughing because you grow older. You grow older because you stop laughing." - Maurice Chevalier

This saying reveals the secret to youth. We do not stay young because of any serum that we buy from a beauty shop, or through any facial exercise. Of course, you may say slapstick comedy can involve facial exercises. Humor, however, changes something within you. It makes you quicker to accept your follies and see the world with a brighter set of eyes. It does not mean that you are stuck with a pair of rose-colored glasses. Some of the best comedians are often thought of as some of the smartest people. They have to read their audience and ensure that the timing is right. They know what humor applies to what situation. So, it means that they recognize the dark side of this world; they are not blind. However, they choose to use a lighthearted approach to life that they incorporate into their private thoughts and also into their interactions with other people. How would you like to inject some humor into our everyday lives? This book has the answers: There is no stage. There is no laugh track. It is about purely being able to make people laugh.

This book will take you and me—ordinary people—and find ways in which we can be a lot funnier. Hey, there is such a thing as charisma that people like to talk about. No doubt, some people are naturally charismatic. That is a given fact. However, anything that is worth trying can be learned. You don't have to fabricate a personality, either. There is always some humor that we can draw from ourselves.

This book will make use of the How to Make People Laugh recipe:

- A dash of charisma
- Buckets full of self-discovery
- Smattering of acceptance
- Heated in learning
- Garnished with stories and experience
- Keeping it clean and nice

All of these ingredients are within every person. None of us can say we cannot go through this journey. All of us should be able to make people laugh, beyond a stage or without the promise of financial returns. You will find out that laughter itself and life of humor are worth all this focus.

Why would you want people to laugh?

1. It is a health booster—for both you and the other person.

The release of serotonin and endorphins provide you with not just a happier attitude but also enhances pleasure while regulating pain. This is why it is a good idea to visit people who are sick and try to cheer them up with jokes. Laughing is also an excellent pastime for those who are at high risk of hypertension and cardiovascular diseases. It is great for everyone!

2. It burns calories.

You burn about 40 calories when you laugh for about 10 to 15 minutes daily. If you are on the other side of the equation, the effort of making someone laugh while also laughing may increase this for a bit. However, you should not forget to do your daily exercise.

3. It lightens the mood.

As a stress buster, joking around with a friend certainly works. Your chest no longer feels tight, and you just give in to the laughter.

4. It boosts your immune system.

Because joking around helps get rid of stress, it helps strengthen your immune system.

5. It helps you bond with other people.

A few jokes among friends, family members, and colleagues can create lifetime bonds. They make people more comfortable with each other.

6. It makes you look more attractive.

Photographers have already tested this theory. When people are smiling or laughing, their whole faces light up. This makes people more attractive. In a way, the laughter also draws you to a person, beyond appearances. You want to spend more time with a person who can make you feel better.

7. It regulates breathing.

Swimming and other cardio exercises strengthen your lungs and heart. However, laughter does have its share in improving the way you breathe. In simple terms, laughing makes you breathe deeper. It allows you to dig deep as your heart rate increases, and your lungs draw in more fresh air.

Even without knowing the science behind the benefits of laughter, people will be drawn to you because of your capability to make them laugh. Making people laugh helps people forget about their problems even for a little while. It makes them bond with you.

Part One – A Dash of Charisma

This part of the book will deal with the mystery of charisma:

- What is it exactly?
- How do you create a likable presence?
- What are the different types of charisma?
- Which type applies to you?
- How do you retain the charisma even with pressure all around you?
- Do you get to express yourself better—through words and gestures—when you are charismatic?
- Would it be easier for you to make jokes when you are charismatic?
- In the end, how do you apply this charisma to your sense of humor?

Let us find out more in the succeeding chapters.

Chapter 1 – What Is Charisma?

"Charisma is a sparkle in people that money can't buy. It's an invisible energy with visible effects."
— Marianne Williamson

You have probably met some people whose presence creates a commotion—a good kind of commotion. They are those who you just have to crane your neck to see and strain your ears to hear. Here is how a celebrity is born and made.
Even in simple scenarios, you will find people such as these. They are the popular kids, but nice ones. Here are those who are almost revered, but nobody cannot blame them for it because they are gracious and not at all unkind. It seems that they have been packaged perfectly as people. Who wouldn't want to be categorized as one of these golden ones?
But there are different types of charisma. Not all of them will make people laugh.

However, all of them can make people notice. You need to be able to make people notice you first.

1. Authority

Some people exude charisma through their sense of authority. They just appear to know a lot. Their bodily movements show self-confidence. For you to be able to express your brand of comedy, you should also be able to convey a sense of authority. Note that not everyone who has a sense of authority can make others laugh. Some can convey arrogance instead. So, you need to be able to juggle being an authority of your topics with being likable. People do not laugh ***with*** someone they do not like. They may prefer to find an opportunity to laugh ***at*** the person instead.

So, being a know-it-all isn't the best way to start your journey to making others laugh. You don't want people waiting for the next chance to laugh at your mistakes. While boosting your confidence is a plus, people laughing at you or avoiding you just may not be the reaction you want. That will doom your goal of making people laugh.

2. Focus

When you make people laugh, it should be about them. You should genuinely care about what they feel. It is not about making you a star of some sort, although it does give you some feeling of triumph when you can do just that.
Focus on the person if you have to. Establish some eye contact without making the other person uncomfortable. By making the connection, you will know just when to drive in the punchline. You should also be able to read if the other person is following your train of thought. Perhaps the type of joke that you are going for only clicks with a specific group of people with a particular set of interests.

3. Kindness

A relaxed person who imbues positivity can project an easygoing type of charisma. Making people feel comfortable first is an act of kindness. Most kind people do not even have to practice being generous; they have the family structure and childhood development that may have encouraged such value. However, people who have not been able to showcase their kindness—perhaps because of shyness—can slowly incorporate it into their interactions with other people.
In kindness, you can also find the humor of the right kind. A kind person will not be quick to use mean-spiritedness as a means of making others laugh. Laughing at someone else's

expense is just meanness. This may make fellow meanspirited people laugh, but it sure does not create a thriving environment for humor. While you want to make people laugh, you should always strive to do so for the right reason and without hurting others.

4. Visionary

Yes, very few people get to be crowned as a visionary in their lifetimes. However, this does not mean you cannot strive towards something akin to it. Think of humor that you like to convey, the kind of humor that you want people to associate with you. Your thoughts identify who you are because they are original. There may not be many original thoughts left in this world today, but your approach provides uniqueness. This is what makes people drawn to you.

Charisma can also be conveyed through some distinctive features. People with charisma have been shown to:

- Exude self-confidence
    - A charismatic person has a lot of self-confidence. He believes in what he is saying or doing, and this is what makes him compelling.
    - You should be able to exude the same self-confidence by focusing first on things that you believe in. It is easier to talk about them or to navigate them because you naturally gravitate toward them.
    - When making jokes, start with people who have the same interests as you. They will be better able to relate, and the banter becomes natural.
- Show an open body language

- A charismatic person has an approachable stance. His body is open: arms unfolded, toes pointing towards you, and face animated with emotion instead of controlled and detached.
- You should be able to open yourself up to people by revealing more about yourself. When you are self-confident, you can do this more.
- When making jokes, gestures and facial expressions can drive them home. On the other hand, you may become well known for deadpan deliveries, if these are in keeping with your personality.

- Tell stories people want to listen to
  - A charismatic person can easily tell you stories that he is passionate about. You can tell from the sparkle in their eyes.
  - You should be able to share personal anecdotes with no fear. People can tell when you are genuine. So, your stories become more accepted. They want to hear more. People usually appreciate those who put themselves out there.
  - When making jokes using personal anecdotes, a healthy dose of self-deprecation is necessary. However, you have to balance it so that it does not show itself as insecurity. People would be uncomfortable listening to someone who appears not to believe in themselves.
- Listen well
  - A charismatic person sees the value in turning the spotlight towards the other person. He knows that he cannot hog the conversation. The other person needs to be able to speak his mind. A steady banter between two humorous

people is quite a pleasure to listen to, compared to one person delivering all the jokes.

- You should be able to find a person who can match wits with you, without any personal agenda or hidden displeasure. It is not matching wits to win over the other person, but just appreciating others whether they are humorous or not. The other person will better appreciate you when they feel noticed and listened to.
- When making jokes, listen to the other person. Listening may just be hearing their laughter or their feedback. It may also be about letting the other person express his character.

What are the biggest threats to charisma?

1. Self-doubt:

When you don't believe in yourself, you may lose your chance at charisma. Charismatic people get a following. You don't get that following when you are not even sure you are worth listening to.

2. Detachment from others

You cannot develop charisma when you cannot even connect with people. Charisma is all about that connection. Someone has to be able to like you or care about what you are doing. Charisma is not just about being good looking, talented, or smart.

3. Self-absorption

Too much self-focus may just be the opposite of self-doubt. Take care that while you are on your journey towards developing your charisma and humor that you also see beyond yourself. Stay humble. Stay connected.

Can charisma start becoming a bad thing?
Too much of a good thing always ends up becoming spoiled. So, yes, even charisma can deteriorate into something unpleasant.

When you become too aware of this charisma, it may go to your head. When that happens, you become the opposite of charismatic —arrogant and unlikeable.

Chapter 2 – Creating a Presence

"Charisma is the fancy name given to the knack of giving people your full attention."

- *Robert Brault*

When you make use of charisma, you create a presence. You are not just any person, you are that funny person. You are that person who usually makes somebody's day.

Have you ever entered a room and have someone look at you with a look of pure happiness? Then, yes, you have a presence. It may be a presence that is acknowledged by only a few, but yes, it is a presence.

What does that mean? If you are a little shy, you may find yourself still having a great time with a select few. You may be more participative in conversations with family and friends, than with any other person. So, you take advantage of that. Practice more interactions within your comfort zone. See what makes people tick. See what makes you relax and let go.

When you are not in the room, do people seek you out? Have people missed your presence just because you are not there for a day or two? If this is the case, then they know that you cannot be replaced. Maybe they cannot put it exactly into words, but they can sense it.

Yes, working towards charisma can be hit or miss, just like comedy —however, the more that you put yourself out there, the more that your self-doubt wanes. The more you let go of your self-doubt, the easier it is for you to relax and have fun. It is at your most relaxed that you can pull off some of the best jokes.

When you pull off a presence, people will always notice you. You do need to gain the full attention of your intended audience if you want them to laugh.

Some people, on the other hand, may not be missed when they are not present. However, they have a certain presence when they do arrive. You know that they are there. They do not have to be loud, but people take notice. They make others want to come closer and check out what is up with them. The clamoring seems to show that they have been missed, after all, emphasized by their presence.

Comedy takes timing. The timing involved here does not only consider your part in the equation; it also depends on just how committed the other person is.

So, this is what happens:

Interact more/put yourself out there → less self-doubt → more confident → more relaxed → more fun → more effective jokes

Chapter 3 – Grace Under Fire

"I learned that courage was not the absence of fear, but the triumph over it. The brave man is not he who does not feel afraid, but he who conquers that fear."

- *Nelson Mandela*

The best-loved people are not just charming when they are putting up a front. For politicians, the most trusted ones do not just pop up when they are expected to be campaigning. Instead, they have always been out there, mingling and doing things that people usually classify as good deeds. Those who have overcome difficulties or are breaking through the glass ceiling are regarded as better, as well.

If you have read *A Little Princess* as a child, there may be a quotation there from Sarah that you may find endearing. The little rich girl conveyed a lot of wisdom when she said that she was good because she had no reason to be mean. According to her, she had no trials to test her. So, she could not help but remain pleasant.

What Sarah did not see here was that she already had enough charm and wisdom to state or simply just know these things at a young age. She may not be a real princess, but she behaves like everyone's idea of one. When she does meet with some trials to test her (stripping of her place at the boarding school, her dad dying, her riches gone), Sarah has proven herself to be above those trials. She is grace under fire. Most charismatic people seem to be above mundane problems. They always seem to know what to do or how to behave.

Of course, it does not mean that these charmers have never had it hard. It is just that they know what to do during their worst trials and tribulations. They may be giving themselves pep talks, even as they see the reality of their problems.

How will this show up in humor?

You may have noticed that standup comics know how to make fun of their troubles. Because they do it so easily without any hitch or sign of sadness, you can say that they have moved on. They not only move on, but they are brave enough to keep on revisiting the issue. They can take the issue and come up with something witty about it. Often, they will include what they have learned during the process of grief and recovery. Motivational instruction is delivered in a fun way. Your listener does not have to feel awkward about the situation. He may even learn something new from your experience.

How should sad events pop up in jokes?

Trials or sad events are often swept under the table. This is understandable. They are not pleasant, perhaps not only for the person making the joke. You can be regarded as insensitive if you proceed without caution.

You can proceed if:

- You are over the event. You don't want to trigger your own emotions. If you attempt the joke while you are still deeply affected, you and your listener(s) may find yourselves in an awkward situation. Can you imagine what your listener will feel if you were to attempt a joke and then suddenly cry? Yes, it is probably just fine—especially if you are among friends or family who understand. This defeats the purpose of making people laugh, though.
- The listener is not affected by whatever problems you want to joke about. While you may be over it, the other person may still be secretly just trying to hold on. This is where your miscalculation may negatively affect someone else. So, hold on right there. You cannot just make people laugh when they are ready. If you want to cheer them up, pick a different topic.

No matter what you do, you should not joke about other people's tragedies. You should not joke about a large-scale event; you would not know if you were talking to someone who is affected by that event. Events that should never be joked about:

- A murder
- A rape
- Jokes with racist overtones
- Jokes with religious discrimination
- Cancer or any other serious diseases
- Terrorism
- People who have lost someone, e.g., a child, a parent, etc.
- People with autism
- People with mental health issues

If you dare try joking about any of the above, that will reflect on you badly. Yes, laughter is the best medicine. You, however, will not get a laugh from such jokes. If you ever do get some wholehearted laughter after making such jokes, be cautious; you may be running with the wrong crowd. There is nothing brave or admirable about jokes that deal with such tragedies and sensitive issues.

When the setup is right, humor is a lighthouse illuminating dark waters. Some say laughter is the best medicine, and they are correct. When you face your problems with good humor, you avoid some of the worst effects of stress: chest pains, developing heart problems, anxiety, depression, and more.

How can humor help you become the grace under pressure you want to become?

Remember, grace under pressure is a sign of charisma. You can overcome your personal troubles through humor.

Humor can help:

- Diffuse tension: Sometimes, you can cut the heavy feeling surrounding you with a knife. People are not sure how to handle the situation. So, you cut it with well-timed humor to ease the tension a bit, without ending up offonding anyone. It is a tough job to do, but when it works, people will be grateful to you.
- Smooth over differences: When you can lead people into laughter, albeit in a gentle, thoughtful manner, you can enjoy camaraderie during that moment.
- Overcome your troubles: Having a sense of humor can help you get out of the rut of the moment. It may not solve your problems, but it will help you become strong enough to face them.
- Analyze your situation: Sometimes, taking on a lighthearted point of view can help you see your situation in a better light. This is when you realize that there is, after all, the cliched light beyond the tunnel.
- Bonding with people: When you find people with the same sense of humor or similar desire to get over their setbacks, you may have found your tribe. People do appreciate being in the presence of someone more optimistic or eager to get on with light. Similarly, two people who wallow in negativity can pull each other down into the mire.

Charisma during troubled times gets a direct lift from a sense of humor. Other people displaying grace under pressure may not always be funny. You can observe some who simply try to be more optimistic about their lives. Instead of simply waiting for others to give them advice, they give themselves advice. They know that the solution is inside them all along; they just need to tap into it. However, they are also aware that there is no more magic cure for grief. They must be able to go through the process slowly but surely.

However, there are some points you need to remember:

1. Never use humor to cover up your true emotions.

Again, you need to be ready. You cannot just think: Oh, I need to joke around so that people will believe that I am fine. Well, are you fine? At least be honest about what exactly is going on inside of you. Are there still some issues that continue to require resolution? Perhaps you need to face your problems first.

While laughter is the best medicine, it is also not healthy to suppress emotions. You have to deal with them first. You need to know whether you should face your issues first. See if you need to talk to someone who can help you manage your emotions.

2. Don't jest about people just because you feel bad about yourself.

Sometimes, it is tempting to put other people down just because you feel terrible about yourself. Do not be tempted. Think about being on the other side of the equation. How would you feel about it? Would you want to get some laughs by putting others down? Being mean to others will make you feel worse about yourself in the long run.

3. Use inside jokes.

The first few people that you joke about your past troubles with are those close to you. They know you enough to understand whether you have moved on or are simply trying to put up a front. Because you know each other well enough, a few inside jokes about that particular situation can bond you for life. The idea of laughing about this little inside joke while others look at the two of you as if you have gone crazy can make you laugh even more.

It is difficult to find humor in tragedy or any other sad situation. Imagine getting fired from your job. You go home, shoulders slumped, and spine bent. You go to your desk, rest your head on your hands. Your elbows seem to carry the whole world. Would you like to joke about what happened to you just then?

Of course not.

The experience is still fresh. You do not know how quite to tackle it. It is natural for you not to feel any semblance of positivity anywhere.

That is normal.

So, you think. How are you going to get out of that situation? Grieve a little, of course. Then, analyze. What happened? Why did I lose my job? Is it me or is it my boss? There are so many possible answers here. Different people will have different experiences.

For example, you may have been fired because of the pandemic. The firing is not due to anything that you have done wrong. So many people have become helpless victims. So, you think: *How can I solve this problem?* That will be your natural frame of mind. There will be no jokes from you for a time. You need to survive first. So, you do—try to survive—by trying to find a job to put food on the table. Later on, having fully survived and thrived, you may find some humor in the details. You may start joking about how you spent nights eating tubs of ice cream that you cannot afford in front of the television. For now, you cannot do that yet.

Chapter 4 – Body Language

"A shoulder clap is more appropriate in a business setting. But the underlying principle holds: touch more than the majority of people would in the same context. It demonstrates comfort, leadership, and conviction in your communication skills."
— Charlie Houpert, Charisma on Command: Inspire, Impress, and Energize Everyone You Meet

Your body language says so much about you. A charismatic person will be more open to others. So, they do not hide behind folded arms and bowed heads.

Remember that part of your charisma has something about how you treat others. How do you look at them? Do you stare at them with animosity without you knowing it? They usually call that the "resting b*tch face." Some do have this face at rest. However, this will not happen if you are truly aware of the person right in front of you. Are you genuinely glad to hear about what they have to say? It will show on your facial expressions and how you talk to them.

The rest of your body will follow suit. When you are comfortable with somebody, your body language tends to be more open. Here are some signs that show you are willing to engage in the conversation:

- A smile or at least an open expression
- Open (unfolded) arms
- Straight back
- Toes pointed toward the person talking to you

The following, on the other hand, may suggest that you are not interested:

- Yawning (blatantly or furtively, but perhaps you just had a hard night)
- Folded arms
- Bored or distant expression

- Slumped back
- Body directed towards the exit, or anywhere else other than the person you are talking to

Sometimes, we don't even notice that we are revealing so much with the way that we move. We may think that we are hiding our feelings just because we are not saying anything, but we are wrong. So, all the while, we think we are sending our intended signals, our bodies are telling the whole truth.

But here is the thing. To be truly charismatic, you need to genuinely like people. Work your charm on people that you like and who like you. That should be easy, right? It could. It may be a little more challenging for those who are on the shy side. However, despite it all, it is more comfortable.

Of course, you have to eventually bridge out and expand. You have to go beyond your comfort zone, but with the right intentions. You cannot just go around, turning up the charm for everyone if you are starting from a very introverted place. Once you do get a feel for mingling with people beyond your usual cliques, you can incorporate some of the following tips:

- Stand and walk with your back straight. Do not let your shoulders slump. Instead, pull them back. Hold your head up, chin parallel to the horizon. You can already feel a little more confident when you do this.
- To further influence your mood and attitude, give a smile to the world. Notice that when you give in to the temptation of just pouting and slouching, your attitude also continues to deteriorate. Conversely, you boost your enthusiasm by starting your day with a smile. Yes, not everything can be perfect every day. However, it is up to you how you should face that day.

- During your interactions with people, make sure that your body language is sympathetic, empathetic, and supportive. People will more likely listen to you when they know that you can do likewise.
- Focus on the emotions of what you are trying to convey. When you do, you are more fully able to express yourself both in words and gestures.

A cliched expression is that "actions speak louder than words." This is true. You can control what you say. You can stop yourself from saying hurtful words, for example. However, it is more difficult to control your gestures. Perhaps you can keep your hands still, but there will be other parts of the body acting out your emotions. Your nose can flare due to disgust or alarm. Sometimes, you just cannot help it. Some also reveal too much by the way that they blush. If you are like this, people can easily see when you are embarrassed. Similarly, some people grow pale when scared or caught.

Charm is all about being as honest in your interactions as possible. Your "audience" would want the genuine article—a person they can look up to or at least relate with. To be truly charming, you need to see the best in people, as much as you can. Interact with them with the real desire to get to know them. Charm is not just about painting yourself well so that others will like you. You need to love being with people. That is how your charm develops.

Part Two – Buckets Full of Self-Discovery

"When you love and laugh abundantly, you live a beautiful life." – Unknown

"A well-balanced person is one who finds both sides of an issue laughable." — Herbert Procknow

You grabbed this book because there is something within you that wants to make people laugh. While you cannot claim that you will change the lives of others by making them laugh, you are attempting to give them a moment they can relish.

Making people laugh also changes you. It begins within you. That desire has sprouted from somewhere inside of you. So, the very first person that you will change during your journey is you.

Hey, nobody is expecting you to behave like a Mr. Bean. It is alright to be a serious person at work or school. You can wipe away that goofy grin from time to time. You don't have to be funny all the time.

However, you have that desire. This desire continues to make you want to make people laugh. You want them to share in your vision of a beautiful life—one that is full of laughter.

So, you begin with your self-discovery. Ask yourself the following questions:

a. Why do I want to make people laugh? Is it a desire that stems from a secret ambition of becoming a comedian, or do I just feel good about hearing other people's laughter?
b. If I make this joke, how will people react? Will somebody get hurt or offended? Will people laugh because they like me or laugh because the jokes are funny?
c. Will I be willing to be the butt of jokes, too? How will I feel about it? If my friends, family, or colleagues realize that I like to make them laugh, will they also make jokes with me or about me?

d. Am I a natural storyteller? Will I be able to pull off a punchline without laughing hysterically? Can I do deadpan or slapstick? Will I have enough range to make people laugh in various ways?
e. Am I an extrovert or an introvert? Will my personality affect the way I deliver jokes?

This part of the book will deal with you, your personality, the types of jokes you like, and the means you plan on delivering your jokes. Specifically, it is divided into the following chapters:

Chapter 5. Making Jokes Based on Your Story and Personality

Chapter 6. Effects of Personality on Jokes

Chapter 7. Delivery Styles

Chapter 5. Making Jokes Based on Your Story and Personality

"Be who you are and say what you feel, because those who mind don't matter and those who matter don't mind."– Bernard Baruch

Writers often fashion their first novels into barely veiled reimaginings of their own lives. This is what they know. So, the descriptions are rich, the events are vivid, and the emotions are raw. They have real-life events to draw these stories from.

After they are done publishing this first almost non-fiction novel, they read the reviews and the regular readers' feedback. Those who clamor for more have been drawn not only to the story but unknowingly to the writer himself. There was a connection somewhere. So, the writer's sophomore efforts may still slightly resemble his first novel. Someone wiser may only copy the style but steer the story away from the possibility of repeating a plot or subplot.

When making jokes, sometimes it is easier to start from yourself, as well. You can start zeroing in on yourself as the focus of the funny vignette. It is safer to do so after all. Sometimes, though, you have to let go of jokes that are too close to home if people start feeling as if you have nothing else to talk about. So, you delve deeper into jokes that your personality feels comfortable with.

Here are some ideas:

- Find funny moments that have happened in your real life. It can be as cute as a Kid's Say joke involving your child or student. It can be a humorous look at an otherwise stressful situation that you have found yourself in.
- Recognize the folly of people around you. Examine why these actions seem funny to you. Is it something that you

can freely joke about without being mean or offensive? Perhaps it is a joke shared by a friend who recognized silliness in his behavior.

- Watch comedy films or listen to standup comics. What type of humor do you easily react to? Are you a person who is difficult to please, or are you someone who laughs at both wry wit and slapstick?
- How about jokes that you have to read? Read the Sunday comic on your local newspaper and check if the humor works for you. Then, compare that humor to the type that you read from *Mad* magazine when it was still being published.
- Observe your life and its many aspects. Are there some particular moments that you normally chuckle to? For example, someone who has a better attitude in life will probably laugh at himself if he finds out that what he has been looking for has been in his hand the whole time. On the other hand, someone who is under a lot of stress will end up throwing a tantrum.

How about making your life abundant with laughter?

- Have more pictures of yourself smiling taken. You want to see yourself at your best. Forget about how puffy your cheeks look when you smile widely. When you smile genuinely, it reaches your eyes—and that is a glorious thing to see. People will more likely want to interact with you when they see such an open expression of happiness.
- Be around people who like funny stuff. They will appreciate a little banter now and then. This will act as your natural means to practice your humor. Be around naturally happy people. They are not perfect. They are not

free from problems and responsibilities, but they know how to look at the lighter side of things.

- Watch a lot of comedy. Not only will you get a good laugh as lung exercise, but you also lower your cortisol this way. With the stress hormone down, you are less likely to crave too many calories. You may lose weight. If not, then at least you have lowered your stress even for about an hour or so. Comedy sitcoms may also provide you with ideas on how to make jokes work in the ordinary world setup. Yeah, they have a laugh track, but at least you will discover what makes you laugh and what makes you annoyed.

To test all that you have read above, you have a little assignment:

1. Watch your favorite standup comic. Take note of his/her best jokes.
2. Do those jokes reflect a moment in their lives?
3. Do those jokes reflect their point of view?
4. Do those jokes reveal a lot about who they are?

Standup comics have to write their comedy routines. They have to draw upon their experiences to write the most effective jokes. After all, these are jokes that they are invested in.

For you to do something similar, you can first BRAINSTORM. Fill the blanks below:

I love _____ so much that I _____!

I hate ______ because ______.

My pet peeve is ______. I just cannot stand it when ______.

The best moments in my life happen _______

I am scared of ______! When I see ______, I ______!

I am ashamed of the fact that ________________.

I am addicted to ___________. I just have to ______________.

When answering the above questions, you are finding possibly humorous situations from your life. However, you don't have to attempt at making them funny right away. You can first fill in the blanks, read the answers aloud to try them for size, and then check your tone.

Are you too serious when you are answering the questions? Do you sound like someone answering an '80s slam book? Perhaps, the answers can be tweaked to make them sound like deadpan jokes.

Are you sarcastic? Do you think you can tweak that sarcasm to be funnier, and not hurtful? Sarcasm may just be your style, especially if this is grounded in your personality. People will know right away that you are just being you.

Are your answers naturally humorous upon close inspection? It seems that you are on your way.

Give it a try. Then, compare what you have with what we have come up with.

1. I love chocolates so much that I have a secret stash in the house I keep away from my siblings.
2. I hate Facebook memes because they usually remind me of jokes that I was not able to tell myself. They speak so much about my life.
3. My pet peeve is a tall man with sweaty armpits. I just cannot stand when I have to commute with one on the subway. I am short.
4. The best moments in my life happen when I am asleep. Seriously! Everyone is like, "Oh, you should have been awake, but we felt bad waking you up!" I am a night shift nurse.

5. I am scared of little toddlers with big grins on their faces. I don't know if I should make sure they are okay, or if I should make a run for it.
6. I am ashamed of the fact that I fart whenever I am nervous.
7. I am addicted to grandma games—you know, not those cool games on PS4 but the ones that require you to buy gems to move along.

Some of the responses above are funnier than the others, but each can be material for your next joke. If the person you are going to tell the joke to knows you well enough, then it becomes an inside joke of sorts. You know when they make that connection when they start grinning widely even though you have not finished the joke. You may also observe the other person nodding in comprehension.

So, don't force it. Upon seeing the fill-in-the-blanks statements, do a few rounds:

First: Just answer. Do not think too much. It is much better to take a response from your reality. It is easier to build a story from something that you know well or believe in.

Second: Examine your answers. Are you a positive or a negative person based on them?

Third: Add details that can make the story vivid.

Fourth: See what happens when you swap the answers to "I love_" and "I hate_," and other opposites.

Another exercise that you can work on is a variation of either FREE ASSOCIATION or the Rorshach test.

You can either take a look at a random set of words or pictures (instead of the actual inkblot test referenced above) and say the first thing that pops in your head. Don't overthink. Don't try to be so cool at the first try. Just say or write the very first thing. You have nobody to fool, except yourself.

What you need:

- A pen
- A pad to write on/sheets of paper
- Random words (You can make someone give you the words OR you can use Charades or any word generator online)
- Random pictures (cut-outs that someone has prepared for you) OR even children's flashcards

You may need a little help because you should not know the random words and random pictures beforehand. Someone can flash you the words or just prepare them for you to work on alone.

Try some of these words on your own:

1. PET
2. HOUSE
3. OVEN
4. FRIEND
5. LIST
6. WORK
7. COFFEE
8. CAKE
9. FIRE
10. SLEEP

How about the following pictures/inkblots? Numbers 1 to 3 are commonly used inkblots in psychoanalysis. Numbers 4 and 5 are non-copyrighted photos of a breakfast feast and a bag, respectively.

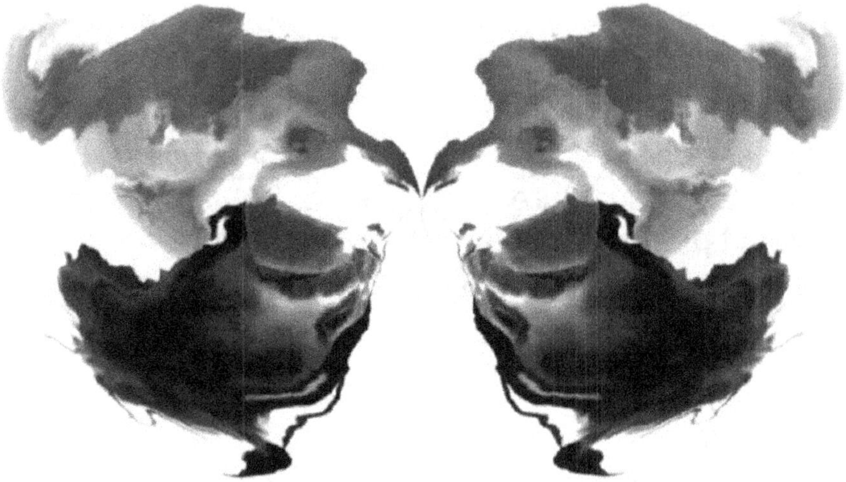

1.

2.

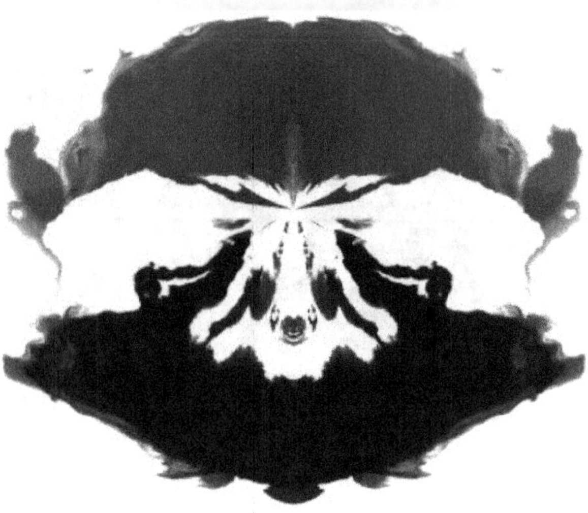

3.

4. 

5. 

Before you read our answers, try doing the FREE ASSOCIATION exercise on the above words, inkblots, and pictures. Again, remember: Be quick. Be honest. Use a timer so that you don't spend a lot of time on each. Finish the word association in 30 seconds. Finish the picture association in 15 seconds.

Possible results:

Each person will have a different set of answers because the answers reflect who he is deep inside.

1. PET – little beloved that does not stop bouncing around
2. HOUSE – not my own

3. OVEN – my stress baking friend
4. FRIEND – virtual
5. LIST – of things I need to do
6. WORK – 24/7
7. COFFEE – my source of life
8. CAKE – a slice for my thighs
9. FIRE - fear
10. SLEEP – barely get any

There is no right or wrong way of answering free association exercises. Sometimes, answers can even stray. This straying reveals a lot about your mindset. You may also not be familiar with everything that will be put in front of you—or you know what they are, but you just do not have much of a relationship with the object or person.

Not all of your answers will be funny, of course. However, all of them have the potential to be expanded.

The first answer above for PET may be expanded to write pet jokes.

Pet jokes can be general. In the joke below, Seinfeld was talking about all dogs:

"Dogs have no money. Isn't that amazing? They're broke their entire lives. But they get through. You know why dogs have no money? No pockets."
Jerry Seinfeld

It could be personal.

"I took my dog for a walk, all the way from New York to Florida. I said to him, "There, now you're done."
Steven Wright

While we find Seinfeld's joke funny, some of us who have dogs that like to walk way too much will appreciate Wright's joke. It feels personal. It becomes an inside joke among pet lovers.

The HOUSE joke may also be expanded. The answer "not my own" can be a little sad. It means the person who answered does not have his own home yet. He is renting or continuously paying a huge mortgage. Whatever the case may be, a joke stemming from this has to rely on the delivery.

What is your attitude about not owning your home?

Yes, ultimately, it can be sad. However, have you decided to see the light side of this situation? You will be surprised at the material that you can get from this one topic. Some people may choose to write a serious commentary about how it is difficult to buy a house in the 21st century. You can follow the same thoughts, but with a lighter tone. You are, after all, seeking to make people laugh. The first step is to make yourself feel good about life, see its positives, despite all the difficulties.

The OVEN response can be expanded. It can play with your obsession with baking. It may offer a little insight into how you go to the extremes when you like doing something. It does not have to be merely about baking.

The FRIEND response can go sad quickly, as the answer suggests that the Improv Partner does not have any nearby friends, just ones that he can contact via social media. It can also mean that he does not have any friends at all, just imaginary ones or ones that he interacts with from time to time online.

The LIST response can support the person's overworked, slightly antisocial stance. Together, the picture is becoming clearer. The funny person's personality is starting to emerge. This is why it is best to brainstorm with several words. You will find that some of them will start making connections.

Similarly, the COFFEE and SLEEP questions further drive the idea that you are a workaholic with coffee as fuel and a sleep deficit as your main problem. The more your materials are based on real life, the better that you can do them justice.

Even the CAKE question can still support a certain lifestyle. People are starting to see you as that workaholic who drinks too much coffee, cannot sleep well, stress bakes, and gains weight, but cannot stop working because the mortgage is up.

You are, in fact, a very relatable person. Others experience most of your struggles. Of course, the exact details may be different, but you can further highlight the similarities.

Because you are making people laugh in your daily life—not on stage—it is easier to know which jokes may be relatable to the person you are talking to. You may have heard the concerns of your work colleagues, friends, and family members. You also have an inkling of what could make them feel hurt or offended. Joking about how you finally earned enough money to buy that home you have been struggling to get may have to be put aside in front of a person who has just lost his job or home.

Now, let us move on to the INKBLOTS and PICTURES.

These are a lot more complicated, but may be effective in discovering who you are and what you are passionate about or scared of.

Try it on your own first. Then check the sample answers below:

1. The first inkblot is of two identical old men fighting.
2. The second inkblot is of two shrimps on a dish—about to get cooked—plotting their escape.
3. The third inkblot is of an enraged French soldier, squinting at you.

4. This reminds me of breakfasts in movies. They are abundant, but they never really get eaten. I volunteer to eat the rest.
5. This reminds me of how my bag carries a lot of what I value in life: wallet, IDs, chargers, devices, pocket change, pepper spray, extra underwear, a slice of a ham sandwich, etc.

The three inkblots can generate a whole range of answers. You may even use inkblots as the main focus of the joke. The joke can see you looking at a wide array of inkblots and saying:

a. Outrageous, detailed answers for each (possibly with backstories)
b. Saying the same thing for everything
c. Dismissing all as inkblots
d. Giving one-liner jokes as answers for all

What was your inkblot test like? Don't worry about sounding a little crazy. You are doing it for fun. However, you should also consider trying to stick to what the inkblots kind of look like. You want your "audience" to say, "Oh, it kinda looks like that. Doesn't it?"

The two pictures included in the exercise may also be used to reveal your attitude towards those objects. They may also paint a clearer picture of what your life is like.

Now, let us move on to creating mini-chunks of your life, otherwise known as TWEET format statements.

As with the FREE ASSOCIATION exercise, you will write without the intention of being funny. You can examine the thoughts afterward to see if there is anything funny there at all or the potential for development.

Tweet Exercise

A tweet can only go up to 280 characters maximum. It is compact and precise. You may be able to write some of your thoughts based on the following:

1. Life in general
2. The state of the world
3. Taking care of babies
4. Teaching someone how to do something
5. Eating whatever you like

Now, try it. It is better to type it on your computer, or even on the Twitter app of your phone so that you can easily tell if it already reached 280 characters.

1. Life in general right now is just about getting up in the morning and letting the rest just happen to me. I have gotten tired of planning things that never happen, anyway. I am letting life grab me unawares now. Well, at least when I am not at work. I don't want to lose my job.

2. The world is still battling the pandemic. So much else is going on, though. This pandemic has revealed a lot more: corruption, mismanagement, poor health care systems, poverty in general, and a lack of trust in the government. We now see a lot of silly horror mistakes in real life.

3. Taking care of babies is much more different than taking care of eggs for a high school project. When you break the egg, you get a failing grade. When you do not take care of a baby, you can risk its life. Its effects are a whole lot more fatal. You won't get over it.

4. I would rather do everything than teach someone something. Well, if I were a teacher, I don't really have a

choice. At home, though, it is easier to cook the whole meal on your own than teach someone to do it. It is not wise, though. That will be teaching someone to be lazy.

5. Eating what you like is only good for the moment. When the calories start making themselves known, you have to do something else that you hate doing—exercise. Exercise and diet experts, I really need your help! This waistline is exponentially expanding.

As you can tell, none of the above has been written to be funny. They are matter-of-fact thoughts of a person. It is not beyond the realm of possibility that some may get retweeted, but usually groundbreaking and hilarious tweets are the ones that get more traction.

How did you do? Did you fare better than us? Did you post them on your Twitter account and get any reactions or retweets?

Tweet #1 is serious. However, it has the possibility of becoming funny if you take a look at the lighter side of it.

This popular meme is a funny interpretation of it. You may have seen variations of this meme on social media.

In real life, people have joked around about their life with friends when they are at their most stressed. The punchline serves as a mood lifter. Though worried, the person making the joke will still go on to do whatever task it is that is causing him stress.

Tweet #2 is a lot more serious. It involves a pandemic that can cost hundreds of thousands of lives—or even more. Not only is it a health issue, but it brought forward some very dark themes. Making a joke about it is going to be complicated. Do not dare to make jokes about the pandemic to:

- People who have lost their jobs because of it
- People who have family or friends who lost their lives because of the virus
- Just about anyone who will keep on passing the joke (The Internet already has a name for the passing on of such jokes for the sake of how it makes them feel to react—emotional contagion.)

So, tweet #2 is best left as a serious tweet. People have to take the situation seriously.

Tweet #3 is serious, as well. It can be tweaked to be funny, but it can be dangerously close to being tacky and irresponsible. Parents may not fully appreciate your jokes unless you are a parent yourself and they know your brand of humor can sometimes go to the dark side.

There is a meme doing the rounds on social media that shows the Dos and Donts of baby care. A particular meme of a hand pulling a baby by the head can be offensive, but darkly funny. The Do parts shows the baby being carried the right way, with hands supporting the torso and the neck.

Some may find it hilarious, but there is a possibility that some may find this offensive.

Tweet #4 can be pretty serious, as well. However, teaching jokes seem to be safe enough to get into. You can find a way to tweak the tweet, which provides you with so much material: teaching, stress, spoiling others, being a good example, impatience, and more.

Tweet #5 has attempted to be funnier than the other tweets. It can still be reworded to emphasize what is going on. This is a joke that is better off done in a self-deprecatory way. Yes, it is better to joke about yourself gaining weight, than involving anyone else. If you joke about yourself gaining weight, you see the lighter side of things.

On the other hand, joking about somebody else gaining weight is insensitive.

Chapter 6. Effects of Personality on Jokes

"Jokes proper thrive in the company of joke tellers." – Agnes Heller, Aesthetics and Modernity: Essays

Now you know where to get some funny material from your personal life. Now, how does your personality affect the delivery of jokes?

It can make or break it.

Heller, in her book *Aesthetics and Modernity: Essays*, has commented that reading joke books are not the proper way to receive jokes. This means she does not believe in how social media memes are being delivered.

What gets discarded when you read jokes instead of listening to them?

- You lose the camaraderie that is formed when the joke-teller and the audience create a bond. As the audience laughs, it shows that it understands the joke as it is meant to be. The same happens between friends or colleagues making jokes at the office pantry.
- You lose the opportunity to witness a great storyteller create a performance, complete with acting, timing, and proper intonation. A great joke-teller knows when to pause, hush, and change his tone.

So, how do you deliver your jokes to your family and friends?

Much value is being given to how a joke-teller delivers his jokes. Your delivery, however, does not have to follow the requirements of a standup comic's own.

For stand-up comics, they have:

- To make the most of the stage that they are on: adding physical comedy and facial expressions that are

appropriate to the joke
- To write original jokes: it would be in bad taste to recycle other people's jokes
- To connect to a big audience

You, on the other hand, can make use of existing jokes and give your twist to it. You don't need a stage, and your setup is more intimate.

What you need to do:

- Be confident about your joke—who will laugh if the joke-teller seems uncertain about what he is trying to say?
- Convey the appropriate emotion to carry the joke
- If you are going to say an existing joke, add your twist or attempt to make it sound better
- Make it feel like an inside joke
- Appeal to the particular person's interests

So, anyone can make other people laugh. Even the shyest among us have some concept of what we find humorous. With likeminded people, these jokes can work well.

Myers-Briggs and their Effects on Sense of Humor

Personality can certainly color the way you make your jokes. So, it is no surprise that the Myers-Briggs can come up with not only 16 distinctive personalities but also with 16 distinctive types of humor.

Half of these personality groups are made up of introverts. Introverts are not exactly what you will think of when you are trying to find some worthy joke tellers. However, they do have their brand of humor. Steve Martin and James Belushi may be famous comedians, but they are also known to be introverts.

There should be more famous introverted comedians out there, but most would not have categorized themselves as such. You would know that there must be a whole group of them because of the advantages posed by being an introverted comedian:

They are more observant. So, they are likely to find material from their surroundings that people can relate to.

- They are empathetic. So, they know when to move on because the audience is not responding the way he intended them to.
- They are more reflective. This means that they can take any subject or situation and analyze each. They can make their conclusions about anything that interests them. They are not simply interested in the surface issues, but also the details. Yes, introverts can be more detail-oriented.
- They can work independently, as well. So, they have no problems with creating their jokes without a whole group of writers. Because of this, the content is even closer to their hearts.

With Myers-Briggs, you can find eight personalities that are considered introverted. They have their unique way of handling humor.

While not all of the eight have specific characteristics that truly identify them over the rest of the introverts, they all have the advantages mentioned above.

You can be sure, however, that the ISFJs will be more aware of other people's feelings. So, they are less likely to make jokes that can hurt other people's feelings. INFJ's sense of organization can produce some well-formed setups and punchlines, while the INTJ's can provide original, creative content. Most of the other introverts are well suited to making genuine connections with their audience.

Now, what about the extroverts?

Most people may think that extroverts have the proper sensibilities to become great comics. They can be because of the way they desire interactions with people. However, you may argue that introverts also love interacting with the people closest to them. This book, after all, is not about becoming a professional comic or standup comedian; it is all about being able to make people laugh. Sensitive people care about how they can make their loved ones happy.

For extroverts, however, it is the norm for them to try to keep on making people laugh and be happy. Comedy or any other human-to-human interaction is their natural setting. You could say that extroverts have fewer inhibitions when it comes to being on a stage or chatting up a storm with a friend.

Extroverts such as ESFPs are friendly and outgoing. These are the friends that will not leave you with any awkward silence between the two of you. ENTPs have the quick thinking needed to make jokes that can adjust to different people. ENFPs have the enthusiasm needed for great physical comedy. ESTJs, meanwhile, will have the efficiency in formulating great jokes with meat. You may expect some blunt, straight jokes from an ENTJ. What they have in common is the ability to bounce with any other person.

An Insight into a Comic's Mind

While the statistics of the ratio of introverts and extroverts in the comedy world are not clear, a lot of studies show that some comics are not as happy or outgoing as they seem on stage.

Some comics, such as Robin Williams, have been revealed to have depression. Jokes seem to be the most fun they have. Others may not have been depressed but were shy or very introverted that they content themselves in being wallflowers in get-togethers. They are usually quiet offstage.

Now, what does this have to do with you?

With making people laugh offstage, it is less complicated. You have to deal with people who may already have a connection with you. So, extrovert or introvert, you already have a unique relationship with whoever it is that you are talking to. You don't have to have extra powers of observation; you will be communicating with someone that you already know.

Introverts will have their friends and family that they can already relate to. Extroverts have several people to choose from (acquaintances, colleagues, and more).

Chapter 7. Delivery/Joke Styles

"My vibe is like, hey you could probably pour some on my lap and I'll apologize to you." – John Mulaney

There are various types of jokes out there. Some, however, can only work on the big screen with effects to support them. Others are better off the stage. How do you then find jokes and delivery styles that will work with your friends, family, and colleagues?

Joke Styles/Types

Anecdotal – What you have been working on in the earlier chapters will mostly fall under this type of joke. This is a comedy that you draw from your personal life. Director Judd Apatow says that comedy improves "as it becomes more personal." Your audience best appreciates your joke when they can see something similar to their own lives. Here is the camaraderie that can occur when jokes are exchanged either through performance or an exchange.

Deadpan – If you are known for being serious most of the time, some people may stop and think: is he joking with me? However, as they start listening more to what you have to say and recognize the pure humor in what you are saying, they will accept that this is the way you deliver your jokes. Seemingly both trivial and nonconsequential in tone, the deadpan delivery can make people laugh a little louder. The contrast of hilarious content and serious monotone can set some off.

Observational - Taking a closer look at everyday situations can provide you with some observational jokes. Anything can be transformed into a humorous observation. However, you must make sure that people can relate to you. If you are going to observe doctors, for example, it will work best among health professionals, their families, or some active patients.

One-liner - The setup and the punchline are delivered in one short, witty sentence. There is no room for hesitation here. You just deliver the whole thing and get the results. On the other hand, a punchline can take some time to simmer before it explodes—and you just may change your mind.

Rick Moranis's character in *Spaceballs* said: "I am your father's brother's nephew's cousin's former roommate." It is simple, possibly factual, but also undoubtedly funny. You don't have to be in a particular demographic to understand this.

Self-deprecating - Are you ready to make fun of yourself? Well, this is where you go with self-deprecating jokes. The joke-teller is, in reality, a lot more self-assured when he can submit himself to judgment and ridicule in a joke. You have to be comfortable with your flaws for you to be able to use them in such jokes. The delivery is also important. It must be clear to the person that you are talking to that you are, in fact, joking. You don't want the reaction to be, "Are you okay?" or "I am here for you." The only reaction you need when your self-deprecating joke is successful is loud laughter.

While self-deprecating jokes are still best delivered verbally, quite a number of tweets have been successful at conveying them.

Twitter has many self-deprecating jokes to offer, coming from celebrities and regular folks alike. The upside to these jokes is that this can boost the mood of people who can relate to the litany of negative traits the joke teller supposedly has. The self-deprecating joke can be in the form of a wordless picture, a one-liner, or a setup and punchline combo.

Part Three – Smattering of Acceptance

"If fate doesn't make you laugh, you just don't get the joke."
— Gregory David Roberts

"A sense of humor is the best indicator that you will recover; it is often the best indicator that people will love you. Sustain that, and you have hope."
— Andrew Solomon, The Noonday Demon: An Atlas of Depression

It is in the acceptance of the imperfect lives that we have that we can find the humor in everything.

Part three is simply a transition. By the time that you have reached this page, you have already gathered enough material from your life, other people's lives, and your own worldviews to be able to make sense of them and find the humor in them.

Part Four – Heated in Learning

"All students can learn and succeed, but not on the same day and the same way."
– William G. Spady

Just like any other skill, making people laugh can be learned. You cannot just give and say the following:

- I cannot do it because I am too shy.
- I cannot do it because I am too hyper and will give up my punchline right away.
- I cannot do it because I don't know how to do it.

Here are some ideas on how you can start trying to be funny (yes, nobody is born funny):

1. Think of things that you find funny.

Think of concepts and existing jokes that make you laugh. Do you smile a bit when you hear them? Do you giggle or do you guffaw? Think about what makes you laugh. Are they the types of jokes that you can share with people you like if they have the same interests?
Then, think of people you are close to who find the same things funny. Perhaps you can deliver some of the jokes that you have come up with or even existing jokes that you have found. Bounce the jokes with these likeminded people. Check how they react to these jokes. Find out what makes them laugh. It would be great if you can find someone willing to assist you with this comedic journey. That person should be able to represent any audience.
However, make sure that you don't make it a point to be funny all the time. Sometimes, when you are not a professional comic, it is better when your audience does not expect your jokes. Of course, you should not insert the joke when your audience is

trying to be serious. However, you can use jokes to cheer someone up.

2. Act dumb. See how it works.

Some comedians get away with making people laugh by simply acting dumb. This is a little tricky to pull off because you must show that it is just an act without destroying the joke. Don't do this all the time, though. People may start thinking that this is your true personality.

3. Exaggerate

Some people naturally exaggerate. However, the results can be varied. Some can end up being funny, but some are just plain annoying.

Think about it: a person who exaggerates to complain is not exactly very endearing. Such a person is labeled as entitled or harsh. Do not be that person.

Have you heard those "Your mama" jokes?

Sometimes, they go like this:

Your mama is so <exaggerated descriptive word> that she <exaggerated comparison, explanation, etc.>

You will find that some may still giggle. However, this is an old hyperbole. People will be amused by it, but will not exactly be filled with hilarity.

4. Tell a funny story

Sometimes, though, the solution to being funny is simple. Tell a funny story. You may ask, "But if I knew how to do that, why would I be reading this book?" Remember, there is always something funny that you see on your daily commute, hear from a young child, or experience in a new environment. If you find it funny, then chances are someone else will find it funny.

What you can do to make the joke work better, however, is to apply actions and facial expressions. Storytelling is always about being able to make the events more vivid to the person who is listening. Your audience should be able to transport themselves to the world that you are imagining.

The world is full of material. Bring a journal when you go out daily. Write what captures your interest. What is so funny about the experience?

5. Use puns

Some people prefer clever jokes. They like playing with words. If you know your puns, then you should be able to come up with all kinds of twists and jumbles.

The stock image has a black background. The white text says, "Bad puns. That's how eye roll". When you use puns, you have to make sure that whoever is listening to you know all the words and phrases that are used to deliver the jokes.

For example, in the joke, "What do you call a cow with no legs? Ground beef," you need to know what:

- A cow is
- Not having legs entails
- Ground beef is

In a picture joke, "I tell dad jokes periodically," the word "jokes" is divided into three parts: JO-K-ES, which represents chemicals in the periodical table. The picture is a great way of delivering this pun joke. However, this does not mean that you can deliver it verbally.

The above are just some of the strategies on how you can jumpstart your making-people-laugh journey. What else do you need?

1. You need a partner that can tell you if you are being funny or not. Since you are not making a career out of it, you can simply try the joke on them. Check their reactions.
2. You need to build more of your confidence. Sometimes, making people laugh is less about the actual material and more about the confidence and hilarity that you are bringing in.
3. It's a good idea to have a book of jokes that you can read for some ideas. Try to practice some of them aloud so that you can hear how they sound. Read the jokes to someone and see how they work.
4. Get familiar with memes that are going around on social media. This way, you are updated with what people find humorous and what they find to be stale and overused.

What is the anatomy of a typical joke?

1. Setup
2. Details

3. Punchline
4. Closing

These parts do not affect how long the joke becomes. Some handle everything in a one-liner, for example. Most jokes only need the setup and the punchline. So, how come you need the above?

Setup – The setup provides you with an introduction. It plays with the audience's assumptions. Some setups are obviously jokes:

- A priest, a rabbi, and an atheist went into a bar… (or any of its variations)
- "Knock, knock…"

Setup is basically what propels the joke. The two examples above can sometimes make some people immediately laugh, and let the others anticipate the next few words.

Anything can be a setup, however. It can be a simple sentence. It is meant to raise an expectation in the audience. If your audience is not biting or has already gone bored from the very setup, then you must be doing something wrong. It is not just the punchline that makes the joke. The setup should already grab your audience's attention. It is what ultimately decides whether the punchline is funny or not.

Here is an example of a setup from a Steve Martin joke:

"I gave my cat a bath the other day."

This perks up the interest of the audience. Of course, this is Steve Martin talking. So, most people will anticipate a joke. If you were the one who started your joke this way, you would still inspire the curiosity of your audience. The other person may think, *Why is this person telling me about his cat?*

Details – Sometimes, a joke needs additional details for the audience to fully appreciate it. However, a good setup may do away with this. Details may be best included in story-type jokes, wherein the joke-teller takes the audience for a ride first before giving the punchline.

In some cases, the details already contain some of the jokes. The audience may have already had a good laugh before the punchline arrives to bring home the point.

The detail may sometimes sound like the punchline, but there is a huge pause plus a certain air that suggests the joke-teller is not yet done with his joke.

Detailed jokes are also delivered in situation comedy (sitcom) shows. The comedians (or rather, the joke writers) have enough time to fill with details. In your case, you can easily use this because you and your possible audience may have had enough knowledge about each other to make it work. Story-form jokes can fall under the four-part joke, as well.

To continue the Steve Martin joke, this is the detail that he added:

"He sat there, he enjoyed it, and it was fun for me, too."

At this point, the other person starts suspecting something, but he is not sure if he is getting a joke or something else.

Punchline – This should be the end of the joke. It should end strong. It must be delivered clearly to avoid the awkward "huh?" moment. This is your ace if you are going gambling. You keep it hidden, but you also give some clues as to what it is about. Then, you deliver it. When you do, people should not be too surprised because you set it up well. You don't want them bewildered. At the same time, they should not go, "I knew it all along."

Two-part joke structures cite this as the endpoint of a joke.

There may be cases when a different punchline can still end the joke well if the setup is rich in meaning and possibilities.

The possibilities are countless, depending on the joke-teller's wealth of knowledge of the topic. He also has to rely on the audience's interest and knowledge of the topic.

Whatever the setup may be, however, if the audience does not "get" the punchline, it is best to leave it that way. If you keep on trying, then you will just appear to be desperate for approval.

Steve Martin ends his joke with this punchline:

"The fur would stick to my tongue, but other than that, it was great."

By this time, everyone knows that Steve Martin's joke persona has ended up licking his cat. The joke can end right here on the punchline, as people absorb and react to it.

You may also dissect the punchline further. Notice that the first part can already hammer the joke in:

"The fur would stick to my tongue..."

The last part can be removed and added to the last part of the four-act structure. This maneuver can be done with a simple pause after the word "tongue."

However, some joke structures still include the fourth part.

Closing – In my humble opinion, a joke must end with the punchline. The audience should be left, still gasping in laughter. The punchline must be strong enough to carry the whole joke. However, some comedians still provide a closing.

Whatever you may plan to do, do not use an explanation as a closing. If your setup is strong and the punchline is driven home, then the two-part structure should have been enough.

However, not all jokes follow a structure. Just like with writing stories, the structure of a joke can also take on a unique form.

Writing a joke is a creative enterprise. Nobody should be able to tell you how you should go about it.

The second part of Steve Martin's punchline can be considered the closing. People are already laughing by the time they hear, "The fur would stick to my tongue." Hearing the comedian say, "but other than that, it was great" may encourage a fresh bout of laughter.

Of course, if you do like to follow a structure to guide you for now, here are some possible "templates."

1. Broken Assumptions

The structure of a broken assumption looks somewhat like this:

Setup: We start with what we assume to be true.

Punchline: Boo! It is not the case. The Steve Martin joke in the four-act structure example is a broken assumption joke. The listeners were expecting that the character was bathing the cat with regular soap and water.

2. Contradiction Jokes

You can probably explain these away as ironic humor. In stories, irony provides a truth that is the opposite of what a character says, a character does, or what the audience knows. In contradiction jokes, this irony is simply made humorous.

a. Words contradict Words

Child A: I did not throw the pencil at you!
Child B: Yes, you did! I saw you!
Child A: No, I didn't. I missed!

b. Words contradict Actions

Alice (calls husband by phone urgently): Bob, you need to drive carefully. There is a madman driving by 43rd Street in the opposite direction.
Bob: You got that right. It is not just one madman. There are several of them, and they have been honking a lot.

This may be best seen than read. Bob is enraged that there are madmen on the road, but he was the one driving in the wrong direction.

c. Words contradict What Audience Already Knows

Person A: Hello. Happy birthday! (with a box containing a mug, shown to the audience beforehand)
Person B: Hi. Come on in!
Person A: How are things?
Person B: Been getting so many mugs for my birthday. I was pretty sure I said I don't need them. I am a teacher. So, I get them all the time!
Person A: Uh-oh. (throws box in the bin) I am much worse. I was so busy, I haven't bought you a gift yet. I will bring it to you tomorrow.

3. Puns/Double Entendres

Puns and double entendres do not necessarily have to be sexualized, but they are often utilized this way. Even with people that you know well, it is better to keep things clean. You don't want to end up with a reputation as someone who likes dirty jokes way too much.

Puns, however, can be a means for you to display your intellect and wit. They can also dangerously go into the corny territory. On the other hand, puns can be paired up with deadpan delivery.

Some puns or double entendres are, however, best delivered via images and will not be good material for you. Well, it won't be recommended unless you are an artist who likes to draw funny stuff to make your friends laugh.

Famous example:

Light travels faster than sound. That's why some people appear bright until you hear them speak.

4. Rule of Three

There is something magical about the number three. Even in fairy tales, we often see things that come in threes. In *The Firebird,* as with many other fairy tales, a king has three sons. The third one is the good prince. It is as if fate has made the king and queen fail twice before finally ending up with an honorable son. This is a very common setup in fairy tales. These are often more tragic than funny, though.

In the world of jokes, the rule of three is also very common. The first two serve as the setup while the third of the series breaks the rule. So, in a way, it is a type of broken assumption joke as well.

Here is a common joke:

Genie: I grant you three wishes.

Man: Great! For my first wish, I want a huge mansion.

Genie: Granted!

Man: For my second wish, I want tons of cash.

Genie: Here you go!

Man: For my third wish, I want you back inside the lamp!

This is so common that many people already expect the punchline. You may twist it a bit when joking around with friends. Perhaps, you can change the punchline to:

Man: For my third wish, I want you back inside the lamp!

Genie: You should read the fine print. (Goes in the lamp, with the house and the cash.)

5. Punchline First

Some joke-tellers like to begin from the punchline. What this means is that they already settled on a punchline that they want to end with. They have decided that it would be funny or even dramatic to end with the chosen punchline. So, they write the punchline first. Afterward, they add the details leading towards the end. It sometimes works if the punchline is strong enough. However, the punchline also cannot save poor storytelling in the setup.

A meta version of this joke is:

The punchline comes first.

What's the worse thing about time travel jokes?

6. Omitted Punchline

When the punchline is very obvious, the joke-teller does not have to say it. He can just make a certain face that suggests what he really means. A successfully omitted punchline joke can be very hilarious. The audience is also thrilled that they are able to get it without it being spelled out for them. This means that the setup must have been very good to make it work.

The punchline has become almost like a requirement to a joke that the image above is a visual representation of how that in itself can become a joke. This is a result of the fact that people still believe that punchlines should always be there somewhere, perhaps in an unexpected form.

Example:

Let's eat Grandma!

For those who are familiar with this joke will know that the punchline is in the punctuation. There is no need to add any other detail. However, some do include a punchline:

Punctuation saves lives.

7. Meta Jokes

Just as there are some meta moments on television and in books, there are meta moments in jokes, as well.

What does meta mean, anyway? It means that it is self-aware and even breaks the fourth wall by talking to the audience.

A joke can be self-referential. For example, it can talk about how terrible a joke it is. This is a joke that will be difficult to pull off on stage, but other forms of the meta-joke can be uttered vocally and still make an impact. An example of such a joke is one that jokes about a well-known joke or joke format. It is like the inception for jokes: a joke within a joke!

Example:

An Englishman, an Irishman, and a Scotsman walk into a bar. The barman looks at them and says: "Is this some kind of a joke?"

The above joke makes fun of a popular joke format, which has three people walking into a bar. The barman here, however, is fully aware of the connotation of having the three men enter the bar.

Even with templates, jokes can still be difficult to write. You have to keep on finding original material. Since you are not going to take it on stage, you are forgiven when you take on even the most obvious jokes—sometimes dubbed as dad jokes—and make them work for you if your personality is just right.

Of course, you may want to provide good material. It is worthwhile to see people laugh at your jokes, with a mix of surprise and appreciation.

Short and Long formats

For some comics, the exact content and specific formats are not that important. They just categorize them as short and long formats.

What is a short format joke?

A short format joke refers to a joke that is told like a knock-knock joke. It is a quick pairing of setup and punchline. You can deliver a whole series of this for a party. Some party clowns actually give several of these short-format jokes while also doing other fun stuff, such as juggling and magic tricks.

For extroverts, sharing short-format jokes with your colleagues should be easier. Sometimes, the joke pairing structure does not require a lot of details. You just get in. You may introduce it as, "Have you heard the joke about so and so?" Then, your colleague will say, "I am not sure. What is it? Tell me the joke." So, you deliver the joke. Usually, it is quick. Sometimes, it can be a little corny. Turning up the charm can help you successfully deliver it.

What is a long-format joke?

A long-format joke relies on a story. You can talk about something funny that happened to you. Within the longer format, there may be a smattering of shorter jokes, which could provide a certain degree of satisfaction along the way to the big punchline.

Tall tales

While both types of personalities can take advantage of the long format, the way they use this format may vary. An extrovert may successfully deliver a tall tale, for example. This is a tale with several bombastic or unbelievable details that usually favor the joke-teller. The obviously fantastical details are often forgiven because they are usually told with a lot of charm involved.

Example:

Three men went hiking. It was their first hike together. It was early in the morning, and they will be going up a steep hill. They plan to eat lunch there. To make things easier, each guy takes turns telling stories, jokes, or whatever they decide to entertain the other two. The first man made everyone listen to his jokes for the first three kilometers. The second man sang many songs that made the other two sing along for the second three kilometers. Now, Leroy, the third man, had to tell stories for the next three kilometers, and they will rest for the last one kilometer. He says he was going to tell a sad story, instead, much to the surprise of the other two:

Leroy: One early morning, a man went hiking with his friends. Six kilometers in, he realized that he left everyone's sandwiches in his car.

You may also make up your own tall tales, based on your personal life. It would be easier to make people care for something that you can be animated about.

Shaggy dog story

Another type of long-format story that an extrovert can get away with, albeit with a few groans at the end, is the shaggy dog story. It is a longwinded story that may involve lots of irrelevant details. Because of its length and sense of adventure, the audience may be fooled to think that there is so much to it. However, it ends with an anticlimactic event, capped off with a shrug and mischievous smile from the comic.

Example:

This example is a variation of the tall tale, but done shaggy-dog style:

One morning, three men went off to hike up a hill. Billy brought five hotdogs, three pencils, and a bottle of coffee. Danny brought a camera, a broom, and a donut. Leroy brought a folding table, a folding tent, and a fork.

By the time they were almost at the top of the hill, they met a witch. They knew she was a witch because she was wearing a pink smock with spiders drawn on them. She also had warts on her otherwise polished toes. She grinned at Billy and asked for a hotdog. She said she could smell them from five kilometers away.

Billy whispered angrily, "Oh, she is really a witch! My mum cooked me these hotdogs!"

Danny: Don't worry Billy, just give her one. You still have four, I have a hotdog, and Leroy has a fork.

Billy begrudgingly did so. The witch was so happy that she gave Billy a folding chair.

Billy: This looks more like Leroy's type of thing.

Leroy: I will take it.

Leroy put the folding chair on his head. On his back, he still had the tent and the table. Sticking out in his pocket was the fork.

The three walked some more and met a fox. The fox welcomed them with a plate where they put the hotdogs and the fork. There were four more hotdogs and a donut left, and the fox was happy with the hotdog.

All four sat by the low table and ate happily. They had a good hike.

The story does not seem like it had a point. You can make it fun by making it seem so much more important than it is, then end it as if nothing was special about it.

Observational comedy

For introverts, reflection and observation are some of their stronger skills. This is why it is good for them to make use of the events and scenes that they have observed in their daily lives. The closer to the truth their stories are, the more likely they will be effective. Here, the story is intimate in the sense that the comic takes a real event or scenario and highlights the funny aspects of the story.

Example:

I love how my neighbors shout at each other every day, throw plates through the window, and then tell us to behave well.

Here is one from Jerry Seinfeld:

"They show you how to use the seatbelt, in case you haven't been in a car since 1965. 'Oh, you lift up on the buckle! Oh! I was trying to break the metal apart. I thought that's how it works.'"

Part Five - Garnished with Stories and Experience

"Life is a shipwreck, but let us not forget tossing in the sailboats." – Voltaire

Your life is rich with experience. Therefore, it is a well of material. All you need to do is to take a little journal and write down some of the most notable experiences for the day. Sometimes, you can immediately recognize the funny bits because it makes you giggle as you experience them. In some cases, though, you have to stop and think about it and then realize—aha! That is the perfect material. I can talk about it—be sarcastic or snarky about it, complain about, be dizzy about it—and a whole lot more heightened reactions to experiences.

So, you may say, but what can I joke about when my life is full of tragedies and mishaps? Well, here is the thing. How you express your story depends on your attitude towards your situation. We have previously mentioned how some famous comedians are depressed introverts. They try to find some humor in their lives to make people laugh and to keep their own moods light.

All our experiences can be material for just about any genre that we can think about. We just need to know at what point of view or angle we should be looking at the details. When there are too many sad events in our lives, we can either capitalize on that and write sad stories that will make people cry. On the other hand, we can take those same events, find the humor in them, and make people laugh.

Let us take a look at this sad and funny retelling of the same story:

1. The sad truth:

I woke up that morning feeling nauseated. I had drunk so much alcohol the night before. I should not have done that, but I still did. It was the fault of that lady calling herself Clara. She was drinking glass after glass, and my boyfriend Chris was looking at her in what appeared to be admiration. I just could not stand them. I will have to fix myself now, or else I may lose my job.

2. Still sad, but funnier:

My head was spinning when I woke up this morning. I could still hear the chirping birds that made a halo around it. If only I could flick them dead so that they would feel what I was feeling and not bother me. I believe I must have cleared all the booze from that bar last night. Yeah, I am a big woman, and I knew that I was not supposed to do that. But guess what? Yes, I did. I downed the Bacardi, Johnny Walker, and even the non-descript gin that old man was nursing in his corner. It was all because of that Clara, who I could swear had sights on my boyfriend, Chris. She was drinking glass after glass as if she was a tube with a hole at the end. The alcohol just seemed to pass through her, seamlessly. Chris was gawking at her with admiration, at how she still looked like she could join a pageant and do a nice little half-wave at all the bar patrons. I could not stand them. They were making my eyes sting—or was that the alcohol? Well, I am forgetting about them for the moment and throwing myself in the shower, or else I may lose my job.

The two scenarios are basically the same. Some may say that the only difference is the personality that each has injected into the narrative. The second one has added some exaggeration and vivid descriptions compared to the first, which is a more matter-of-fact version of the same tale.

Is one of the two narratives a lie? No, both of the stories are truths. However, the first one sparsely narrates the events, while the second one highlights the ridiculousness of the situation.

Now, what about this other scenario?

1. David has insomnia. Every night, he has to struggle with himself. Whenever he sees the sun is about to set, he starts becoming anxious. So, he goes through a whole ritual of taking that warm bath, drinking milk, and winding down. He stops watching television and checking his phone by 8 pm. Somehow, he still ends up wide awake in the middle of the night. He does not want to wake his wife, Emily, up because he knows that she juggles work and cares for the kids all day long. He does not want her to fly into a rage when disturbed.

2. David has insomnia. He has not been officially diagnosed, but he knows he has it. Every night is a battlefield. He practically trembles whenever he sees that the sun is about to set, like some sort of reverse vampire. So, he goes through all the typical ritual steps that are supposed to make him sleep: warm bath (check!), drinking warm milk (check!), and winding down (check!). He stops watching television and checking his phone by 8 pm. So, he ends up watching TV-14 shows and the news. He is like a kid trying to discipline himself into sleeping early. The sad thing about all this is that he still manages to be wide awake in the middle of the night, eyes so wide somebody must have supported them with matchsticks. He does not disturb his wife, Emily, because she juggles so much during the day already. He would instead stare at the ceiling the whole night rather than do so with Emily grumbling in his ears, too.

Again, the two are the same stories. David is still in a lot of distress in both. The storyteller and the reader are the ones getting some fun out of the telling. If David's story ends up becoming filmed, the first one will make it out to be a sort of existential drama while the second will showcase it as a comedy of manners or exaggerated misfortune kind of tale.

What the two tales that we have looked at so far have in common are the following:

1. The second tale is always more detailed. It stretches some parts to highlight them.
2. The second tale is exaggerated. It takes the little humor of mundane life from the first one and squeezes as much as it can from it.
3. The first tale is matter-of-fact, like the objective retelling of a series of events.

What have we learned from them so far?

To make something funny out of your life experiences, you just have to find the details that you can exaggerate, highlight, and pull a little more. Yes, most of these scenarios will not be a funny laugh out loud, haha kind of humor, but you can add in wit. If you can still see wit even in your saddest tales, then you are not down yet. There is a fight in you. You need that fight to make sure that you can make others laugh. Make yourself laugh first. Heck, maybe let out a small giggle or even a knowing smile.

Exercise:

Now, it is your turn. Below, you will see some moments that are typically sad or mundane. Write your first and second version of the following:

1. Waiting at the doctor's reception for your appointment
2. Queueing for milk at the supermarket when the line is extra long

3. Getting fired from a job you did not want, anyway
4. Finding out that the refrigerator has nothing left to eat inside
5. You discovered that your friend has been lying to you about something

You can try your storytelling prowess if you cannot relate to some of the instances above. If you have not experienced any of the above:

- Think of your most boring, redundant experiences (e.g., commute, going to the market) and write about those instead.
- Pick the most stressful event that you have experienced recently.
- Share about your more recent sad experience that you have moved on from

Give yourself time. You are not expected to write everything in two hours, for example. It may take time for inspiration to strike, especially for the second, funnier variation. Do not share bitter experiences that you have not gotten over. It will be counterproductive. You are trying to find material that can help you make people laugh.

Now, what if I write #1 for each of the situations in the first section? Would you be able to write a funnier version now?

1. Waiting at the doctor's reception for your appointment

I arrived at the doctor's office at 9 am. I had an appointment for 9:30 am, but I liked being early. Not really expecting to get called right away, I decided to read some magazines first. At 9:25 am, I straightened my back a little, waiting for the secretary to holler within five minutes. Then, by 9:30 am, the secretary called a person who came after me. I was perplexed.

The other patient headed straight into the inner room where the doctor was, and I was left outside, slightly bewildered. I approached the secretary to ask what has happened. She gave me a slight shrug and said, "That patient is in a lot of pain." I recalled how the patient sat on a chair across me, back straight and smiling a little. He did not look like he was in any kind of pain.

2. Queueing for milk at the supermarket when the line is extra long

I did not like going to the supermarket. However, I needed some milk for my cereal. So, I decided to go. It was still early. I did not expect the line to be so long, but I needed my milk. I already made a lot of effort, walking three blocks just to get to the supermarket. To my dismay, I saw a lot of the people in the line have full carts of food and other stuff.

3. Getting fired from a job you did not want, anyway

I received a memo from my boss. I already suspected what it could be. Because of the pandemic, we were already warned that this could happen. However, it was still a shock when it did happen. I hated my job. There was so much stress attached to it. My hair was prematurely growing grey, and I could barely sleep at night because of everything that it had put me through. However, I also needed to put food on the table. Now, the break happened. It was just devastating.

4. Finding out that the refrigerator has nothing left to eat inside

It was midnight when I heard and felt my stomach grumble. I went to check the refrigerator to get a snack. I usually had a glass of juice to tame my cravings. To be honest, though, I would rather put together a huge sandwich for ultimate satisfaction. That night, though, I could not do either. The refrigerator was empty for some reason. I could swear I bought some stuff just the other day.

5. You discovered that your friend has been lying to you about something.

My friend could not look me in the eye when I asked him about whether he lied about being sick. I found out that he was at a party the night I asked if he had time to talk. I was very depressed at that time and needed a ready ear to listen. He immediately made excuses, but I was in no mood to listen. I just left him there, while he was still talking.

For your guidance, we also prepared some #2 versions. You may read through them to see how they fare against yours. Of course, your work can be funnier than our versions. Some people are naturally inclined but just have not tried creating their material.

1b. Waiting at the doctor's reception for your appointment

I rushed to the doctor's office as usual because I hated being late. I was there at 9:00 am, 30 minutes early for my appointment. I cozied up for my wait with some magazines. By 9:25 am, my slumped back became straighter. I did not want the secretary to call me while I was drooling on a magazine, bored fast to sleep. But guess what? At 9:30 am (my appointment!) the secretary dared call somebody else's name. I was perplexed. This smug-looking man in a suit made a beeline for the doctor's office, chin high as if fully aware that he one-upped me. I was left outside, my mouth wide open and my shoulders trembling with anger. I approached the secretary to demand an explanation. She gave me a slight shrug that seemed to say, "Oh, you don't know how this works, do you?"

She said in that bored monotone, “That patient is in a lot of pain.” I stared at her as if to challenge that answer, but she was deep in her magazine. Here was somebody who would not care if I caught her drooling on her reading material. I remembered quite clearly that Mr. Suit and Pants was not in pain at all. He was just sitting across me, back ramrod straight as if he was trained with books on his head. He had a smile on his face as if he was thinking of something funny. I suspected that he was laughing at me all along.

*The second version is longer and possibly exaggerated, just like a tall tale. More of what the narrator was feeling was added. Sometimes, our unedited versions are funnier.

2b. Queueing for milk at the supermarket when the line is extra long

I loathed going to the supermarket. However, milk for my cereal was an absolute requirement. I would not dare dive into my breakfast without it. Suffice it to say that my day would be bust without any milk. So, I decided to give the supermarket a go. It was still early, and the supermarket was not too far away. I would not drive my car to places too near. Also, I would not have to carry much. I just needed my milk.

Lo and behold! The line was so long I could swear it had all the people in my building, and I lived in a 12-story building with four apartments on each floor. What was worse: each buyer had as many random objects in their carts as my apartment!

*The exaggeration here stems from frustration, just like in the first one. People who are frustrated and in a lot of stress can describe an event in a way that they do not usually mean to be funny.

3b. Getting fired from a job you did not want, anyway

I hated my job. Everyone knew it. So, getting fired should not hurt as much, but it did. When I got the memo, I already had an idea of what it was. Our boss gave us a heads-up at the beginning of the pandemic. But it was still a shock to know it for sure—I was fired!

Now, what was my job like? It was horrible. It was stressful. My hair was turning prematurely grey that I wished it was at least Cruella de Ville fashionable, but it just spelled out old hag. I was thirty-four, you know, but my niece was suspicious every time I mentioned my age. She claimed that she could swear I had my thirty-fourth birthday ten years ago. I wanted to give her a discreet pinch. Anyway, the job not only made me look grey before my time, but it also put me through insomnia hell. After getting fired, I found myself more than willing to go through all nine circles just to get back the job that helped me put food on the table.

*Not all the details in the second version were in the original. Sometimes, a rewrite can inspire you to write more information about the events, especially those that you did not feel was appropriate to the more somber mood of the original.

4b. Finding out that the refrigerator has nothing left to eat inside

At midnight, I felt—and heard—my stomach grumble. I tiptoed to the refrigerator to get a snack. A glass of juice was usually enough to ease my cravings. If I were to be completely honest, though, a large sandwich would be preferable. That would be a ham and cheese, with lettuce bits, thank you! My mouth was watering, and my stomach was expectant, but I was in for a shock. There was nothing in the refrigerator—at all!

*This was not a lot different from the original. The scant material can benefit from being performed. This tall tale is

something that you can narrate to your friend with eyes wide in shock and horror. You may further exaggerate if you prefer so.

5b. You discovered that your friend has been lying to you about something.

My friend looked guilty. If he could put his hands over his eyes, like a kid playing peekaboo, he would. He was that guilty. Of course, he knew he could not avoid me altogether. So, here was the thing: I found out he was at the party while I was crying my eyes out. I was bawling over some girl, and he was at a party with lots of girls. I called him that night, but he said he was too ill to come over. It seemed that the raspy voice with a slur was due to all the vodka he downed. Yeah, he was probably right. He was too sick to talk to me that night—he could barely control his tongue. My ex-friend started giving out excuses, but I was fed up and a little bit jealous that I was not invited to that party. I left him there, mouth hanging. I guess he was still sick because he was trying to get that tongue to work. I was not going to listen.

*The pettiness could be heightened up a notch to make the joke work better for some people.

So, how was your other exercise going? You have now come to realize that making jokes is just like writing stories. Here are some things that you need to remember:

- The more vivid the joke is, the better the impact.
- The more familiar the situation is to the audience, the more that they can relate.
- The setup should be well done. Do not just focus on the punchline.
- Stories that do not have a punchline can still be funny, but you will need to exaggerate, add details,

and even act it out for your audience.

Part Six – Keeping it Clean

"We've begun to long for the pitter-patter of little feet, so we bought a dog. It's cheaper, and you get more feet." - Rita Rudner

In this chapter, we will be looking at why we should keep jokes clean. Strangely enough, there aren't a lot of quotations that promote clean jokes. However, various jokes are labeled as clean.

The above quote remains wholesome, although it goes against expectations, as well. Families can be diverse, but jokes that should be directed to them should be the same in the sense that they should remain clean and suitable for all ages.

Whoa. Let us take a breather.

How do jokes flow?

- A regular pun or joke has rising action in the middle of the joke. Then, the action goes down smoothly.
- A self-deprecating joke rises early. Then, it goes down and it simmers down on a plateau.
- An offensive joke has a long starting plateau. Then, it peaks near the end and suddenly goes down.
- The passive-aggressive joke peaks, plateaus, peaks again, then goes down near the end.

It seems that the jokes that leave a lot of tension at the end are the offensive jokes and the passive-aggressive jokes. An inoffensive punchline helps you relax right after.

Remember that you are making material to make people laugh, not on the stage but in real life. You will be dealing with people like your family, friends, colleagues, and other people that you regularly mix with. So, doesn't it make perfect sense that you should keep things clean?

Yes, it does.

You don't want to earn a reputation for making off-color jokes. Some comedians get away with it. People who like those kinds of jokes can watch their movies or their stage shows. So, it is a matter of choice in that case. With everyday jokes, however, you need to keep it clean and safe for everyone else.

What is a clean joke, anyway?

A clean joke is one that does not make use of profanity and sex to make people laugh. Jokes that make use of profanity usually depend on the shock factor to make the story hilarious. Some are too dependent on the obscenity that it becomes part of the punchline.

Just think about it. Some people hear a little toddler cursing, and they start squealing with laughter. It can be funny, true. We don't have to be completely unaffected by these jokes. However, if you dissect the content of the joke, was there really a joke? It was just profanity for the sake of laughter at the ridiculousness of the situation.

Others rely too much on sex to make their joke sell. Innuendos are used to make people feel giddy about the setup. People may laugh nervously because they know that they are tiptoeing on a taboo and somehow getting away with it. On the other hand, some people let out guffaws because sex sells easily. It seems that the only way to discuss sex nowadays is through a joke or a blatant display of sexuality.

Here are some of the reasons for keeping your jokes clean:

1. It is more difficult to come up with material that does not cater to popular strategies, such as adding cursing and sexual content.
2. Clean jokes tend to have more substantial and well-thought material.

3. Clean jokes will not put you at risk of being sued for sexual harassment. You are now in the "me too" world, where the spotlight is shining on sexual harassment, whether you are male or female.
4. Clean jokes, even if they border on being corny, overused jokes, can bring a whole family together. You want a joke that even the kids can appreciate.
5. Clean jokes will not get you in trouble at work. You don't want people to think you are a pervert of some sort just because you mentioned a couple of off-color jokes.
6. Humor is meant to built camaraderie and trust. Dirty jokes are not supposed to be the means to bond.
7. Humor helps people relax. Adding material that can cause friction inside the office or home is not the way to help people relax enough to laugh.
8. An upbeat, happy atmosphere can improve productivity at work. It is best to keep the jokes tasteful, though.
9. Clean jokes help you gain more friends. They are safer and more comfortable to relate to.

Taking out the curse words and sexual content is not enough, though. You should also avoid jokes that may cause friction between you and the rest. These jokes can also reflect poorly on who you are as a person. After all, what makes you laugh says so much about you, as well.

- Do not joke about race and nationality. This topic is a very sensitive issue, no matter what era you are in. Such jokes can reflect poorly on you as a person, no matter how much you claim that these are just for fun. They show that you tend to differentiate by race or at least have the means to perpetuate stereotypes. In today's political climate, you may even lose your job if you go by this way.

But that is not the real point, is it? You may have to do some soul-searching if you still find race jokes funny.

Not all jokes that mention nationalities are offensive. The Three Rule joke that involves an Englishman, a Scottsman, and an Irishman are just using the nationalities as markers. They could be anyone from anywhere, and the joke will remain as is.

- Do not joke about religion. Some people are indeed freer with these types of jokes. They may even tell you to lighten up. However, people who can make such jokes more likely have an agenda. Are you ready to be part of that agenda? If not, then stay away. Yes, you will not believe all the religions and sects that are out there, but you must show some respect. Even cults have to be taken seriously. They destroy lives, and should not be taken lightly at all.

Some jokes are best delivered by the people involved in the joke. What does this mean? It means that if a Catholic person jokes about the Catholic religion based on what he knows about it, then it is more acceptable. The material comes from his personal experiences, and it is not meant to put down Catholicism. The joke may just be a means to highlight some of the hilarity he encounters as a believer.

- Do not joke about politics, unless you are ready to lose a few friends. You can post your political beliefs online if you like, but they are not something that you should use to make people laugh. Some may, if they agree with you. Others will not because they are on the other side. Even people who may be on the same political side will still refuse to be part of such banter.

As with religion, jokes that involve politics can only be made among people on the same side of the fence. However, sometimes it is best not to do so because politics can dim the happiness of a gathering.

- Do not stereotype. People do not like it when they are limited and generalized using a few characteristics. It does not matter if the group you are stereotyping is represented in your clique at work or elsewhere.

The point is when you are making people laugh, you should not end up in dangerous territory. Some topics are best left alone, especially if you are trying to have some fun.

As people become more focused on being politically correct, you will find that more topics are becoming off-limits. For example, sexuality and gender jokes will offend certain groups of people. Moreover, jokes about stress and death will hurt people who are suffering from mental illnesses. You may find yourself walking on eggshells wherever you go.

The best thing that you can do is:

- Deliver jokes to people that you know well enough.
- Know what makes your friends, family, and colleagues tick. What are their interests? What are their pet peeves?
- Err on the side of corny and overused than go by way of politically incorrect, sexualized, or full of swear words. If you come across as stale, your audience may still laugh, possibly at you. At least they won't think you are a pervert or any other dubious person they should stay away from.
- Remember that you will be joking to a particular person or group. There is something more personal about it. So, don't color that relationship with something you cannot take back.

When you avoid offensive and dirty jokes, you make your jokes inclusive. So what if your jokes are not considered funny by some groups? There will be others who will appreciate them. Maybe you are more adept at interacting with children, for example. Some primary school teachers find it easier to joke around with their pupils than with adults in their circles. Others may be great at joking with friends but are uncomfortable with taking the humor home.

It happens.

You cannot please everyone. However, do not try to please everyone by throwing your morality out the window.

You are a would-be real-life comic. You are supposed to make people feel happy and light, not offended, angry, defensive, or sad.

Part Seven – Improv Comedy

"In improv, there are no mistakes, only beautiful happy accidents. And many of the world's greatest discoveries have been by accident." – Tina Fey

What we have been attempting to accomplish all along is to come up with improv comedy material to make people laugh. Standup comics use improv comedy to bounce around some content with other comedians or even with the audience. These are mostly unscripted jokes that are fresh but not obnoxious. You can tease, but you are not supposed to take it personally.

Why do you need to study improv comedy?

So, yes, you have no ambition of becoming a professional comic. You just want people to think of you as funny. Heck, you just want people to be happy around you. You want to stop spilling out the same serious or awkward talk that has been plaguing your social life.

However, great conversations and awesome jokes do not just come out of nowhere. They have to be either planned or sought continuously and practiced.

1. You will be attempting to make a person laugh. This real person may be a family member, a friend, or a colleague for years. Still, you cannot claim to read their minds. Yes, you will have more success trying your jokes out with familiar people, but your chances are less than perfect.
2. Practice makes perfect. People practice making speeches so that the delivery comes out as seamless. The same goes for improv comedy.
3. You may not know all the reactions to your jokes. However, you know how you can frame your jokes. You are aware of the approach and the possible responses.

Deep inside, you gear yourself up even for the most unexpected reactions.

4. One of the most important aspects of themselves that improv comics have to prepare is their emotional intelligence. The more they are capable of "reading" other people's facial expressions and gestures, the more that they can respond appropriately.
5. You have to be open and comfortable enough to make the banter flow between you and your audience. The more you tighten up to hide something, the more that you are not able to respond freely and continue the humorous conversation.
6. Make it fun. Think of it as a game. It is like a prolonged mental exercise that also makes you laugh a lot.

Why should you focus on the other person?

When you are making someone laugh, you focus on them. Don't dwell too much on how you were not able to deliver your material as planned. That happens. Do not force something that is not happening at all. Instead, take cues from your audience.

Are they bored? Do they look like they just want to check on their phone? Think back. What was it that made your audience turn to you and smile or laugh? Pursue that line of thought. If nothing is happening, let it go graciously and gracefully. You don't want to gain a reputation for being a try-hard comic. Fix up your material for another day. Make the joke slither indiscreetly at first, incorporated in normal conversation.

Are they trying to tell you something? Listen to them. While you may have planned to say a joke from setup to punchline, your audience is key to making that successful. If your audience is more interested in pitching in an idea or two, let him do so. You never know: his ideas may fit right into your joke. This new turn may be the beginning of pure banter. If, however, he has changed paths a bit, you can try to follow him onto his road, then see if you have a way to connect what he said to the rest of your joke. If he is playing the polite audience, he has meant to make a connection somewhere himself.

Are they saying "yes" or "no" to your questions? If your improv comedy skit involves asking the audience, then you have to anticipate the possible answers. It is like creating a flowchart to see where the conversation leads each way.

Whatever the case may be, you should check on what direction your audience wants to go. You are the one who started the banter. You are the one who wants to make your audience laugh. So, it is your responsibility to prepare yourself for anything. You need to be able to gauge the direction in which your audience wants to go. Good improv comedy relies on having the same goal and direction.

Why should you ask specific questions?

While your audience is the focus, the brunt of the comedy weight still rests on you. You are the one who initiates the interaction. So, you have to give detailed questions. This way, your audience knows where the conversation is going.

You can also start with a more general question to see where it will go for both of you. You especially need this if you are dealing with a person you are not particularly familiar with yet. Yes, you may work with the person five days a week, but have you gone into a conversation with him?

- You: What do you like to eat?
- Audience member: Well, just about anything.

You can get some material from that response unless it has completely gone another path from what you were trying to achieve.

While leading statements are not allowed in court, they are especially useful in improv comedy. With leading statements, you get more detailed responses that you can work with.

- You: I bet you like to eat pizza.
- Improv Partner 1: How did you know that? Yes! I love pizza!
- You: Do you like pineapples on them?
- Improv Partner 1: No way! I said I love pizza. When there are pineapples on them, that is just disrespect to real pizza. That is a mutant!

OR

- You: I bet you like to eat pizza.
- Improv Partner 2: No! Not me. What made you say that, though?
- You: I don't know. Everyone likes pizza.
- Improv Partner 2: Not this person, no way. It is fatty, full of calories, and just too greasy for me.
- You: What if I can get you a non-greasy pizza?
- Improv Partner 2: Oh, really? No. Still a no.
- You: But you are Italian.
- Improv Partner 2: Italian-American.

The conversations that ensue after the leading statement contain more information in a short period compared to asking a vague, general question.

Why should you ask for/give a lot of details?

As with the previous question, asking for and giving a lot of details will provide you with the material. You don't want any dead air between you and your improv partner. Even when the content is not funny yet, the mere act of bombarding the other person with questions and getting quick but detailed answers will at least elicit a fascination from the rest of the audience. If it is just the two of you, you will find the humor in the fast exchange.

Let us compare Set A and Set B:

Set A:

You: What is your name?

Improv Partner: Stacey.

You: Where are you from?

Improv Partner: New York.

You: Who do you live with?

Improv Partner: My family.

The first Improv Partner seems bent on just sticking to one word or two-word answers. You get information, but not detailed ones.

Set B:

You: What is your name?

Improv Partner: Stacey Stevens from HR.

You: Stacey Stevens from HR, where are you from?

Improv Partner: New York City. Okay, not really. I just like saying that because I work here in New York, but I have to commute from New Jersey. I wake up very early!

You: Who do you live with?

Improv Partner: Oh, you don't want to know. It's the whole bunch: my mom, my dad, my brother, my sister, and my sister's friend who has managed to not go back to her own place in like three months now.

With Set B, you have gotten more information that you can work with. You can use the information that you got to fill in more blanks. Let us take a look at Set C.

Set C:

You: What is your name?

Improv Partner: Stacey Stevens from HR.

You: Aha, Stacey Stevens from HR. Now, I know who to go to when I want to complain about Bob (make sure Bob is your friend) who has been badgering me with his Tik-Tok videos.

Improv Partner: Yes, you can go to me, or Bob can just show me his Tik-Tok videos.

You: Where are you from?

Improv Partner: I like saying I am from New York, but I actually have to commute from New Jersey early in the morning.

You: Wow! I don't know if I would be able to do that. So, I am just lying down on the floor of Bob's apartment until I can afford my own place.

Improv Partner: I am pretty sure you are kidding!

You: I am not. Who do you live with, by the way? Is it someone who snores like Bob? (Make sure Bob can hear this; wiggle your eyebrows at him to show him you are kidding.)

Improv Partner: I bet I can beat you there. I live with my whole family: mom, dad, brother, sister, and sister's friend, who just would not leave the house. We are a rowdy bunch. I am pretty sure you have a much better time at Bob's.

Because this is improv, the conversation can go in several possible directions. It can also fail.

Here are some possible reasons it can fail:

- Bob is not in the mood to be the butt of jokes.
- Stacey is not as chatty as presented in Sets B and C.
- Stacey may be friendly, but she may not have a lot of material to work with. So, you have to help her along.

Here are some possible reasons it can succeed:

- Your friend Bob can add to the banter.
- Stacey may just be a funny girl herself.
- If Sets B and C are made possible, then you can make her laugh, or at least giggle.

Asking a lot of questions and providing several details together provide you with the opportunity to command most of the content creation. Yes, co-creation is vital to improv. However, remember, you are going to apply this to real life. You will be talking to people who are not primarily in with the joke. Perhaps they are not even comfortable with their sense of humor.

However, when you supply the world in which the conversation will exist, the person you decide to include in the improv will generally know what to say or do. What can destroy this is the other person's complete unwillingness to participate—which brings us to the next question.

Why should you need to know a little background of your Improv Partner?

You must have some idea what your Improv Partner likes. Just like a salesperson, you should be able to read his cues and body language. Before you even attempt to engage in banter with this person, you must know a few things about his likes and dislikes. If the person responds with a sharp "No" or a "not really," then your prospects to continue the improv work are nearly dead on arrival.

The power of listening and observation can help you here. Instead of getting offended by some of the responses, listen. Perhaps, you are the one who missed the joke. Probably, you are talking to someone who has a slightly sarcastic, or even acerbic sense of humor.

Why should you keep creating motion?

Before answering this question, let us clarify that motion in improv does not always mean physical movement. It can also refer to other types of motion. Let us explore every kind of motion:

- Movement from one topic to another

Good improv will not survive if you stick to one topic throughout. No matter how funny the beginning is, it will get old. Imagine talking about the weather—or maybe a burger—for several minutes. Will humor survive?
You: You look like you enjoy rainy weather. (Observing the improv partner's fashionable raincoat, boats, etc.)
Improv partner: Why yes. Oh, you've noticed my attire today?
You: Yes, it looks like you have been praying to the rain god to give you some showers.
Improv partner: How else will I get to wear these?
While there is a possibility that you can continue this line of banter, it may start getting old after the two responses that you got.

- Movement from one place to the next

You can move from one place to the next. Sometimes, the talk is dynamic and physically active. So, you and the person you are talking to are moving from one location to the next.
Because the location changes, the narrative can also change. You can use the environment to give you cues.

You: Hi, do you always walk this fast?
Improv partner: Yes, I do. I am always in a rush.
You: So, it will be okay with me to talk to you as long as I walk fast?
Improv partner: That's right.
You: Oh, look. They opened a new shop. That looks something that you may like.

Improv partner: Wow! A new gadgets store. How do you know?
You: Well, you have the latest ear pods on and a charging backpack.
Improv partner: You have sharp eyes.
You: I adapt. I need something to quickly catch what you have.
Improv partner: Well, here we are. This is where I work.
You: Are you sure you are not the one who has the keys to open up?
Improv partner: No. I may be fast, but Edgar right here practically lives in the office.
You: Hi Edgar!

- Movement in terms of gestures

Without becoming a slapstick version of yourself, you can add animated gestures to make the conversation more vivid and fun. The younger your audience is, the better this will work. Improv work with kids may require you to act sillier than you are usually like.
With kids, you may be able to make them laugh even without words. You can use some improv games with them, somewhat similar to "Simon Says."
There are many variants out there, but you can start with either "Simon Says" or "Frozen." It may work best if you have a group of kids right in front of you, instead of just one, although it can also work with only one child.

You: Simon Says jump. (Jump but do so in a very exaggerated manner.)
Child(ren): jumps and tries to do the same exaggerated movements
You: Simon Says close your eyes
Child(ren): close their eyes
You: Simon Says: open your left eye

Child(ren): open their left eye (Some may struggle with this a bit, making the whole situation funnier for them.)

Frozen is a sneakier version of Simon Says. The kids will be asked to roam around the room and do whatever they want. Approach one child and tell the child to freeze. Then, freeze, as well. Do so with an amusing expression or pose.

The other children who see that someone has already frozen will stop moving. Some will attempt to follow your silly approach. Some will fail at this because they will already start laughing. Others will see that some have frozen and will try to stop moving, as well.
The success of this game is relative. You may find it successful if everyone gets to stop moving—or you may find it successful if everyone fails at that and starts laughing. It is a win-win situation.

- Movement in terms of purpose

Your purpose should also change. If you start the improv sketch with interrogation, it may get old if you continue with that train of thought even after several minutes. You may want to change the purpose or switch roles.
After asking a few questions that establish the person's character and preferences, you can switch roles. This switch is easier to do if the other person is intent on asking you questions, as well.
Another way to move from one purpose to another is to start commenting on what the two of you should do in your free time. You may also suggest a game. The decision will depend on whatever link the two of you have managed to establish during your earlier conversation. You do have to engage them in activities that they will be interested in and have time for.

Being able to read your improv partner will make things a lot easier for you.

- Movement in terms of characters

Sometimes, while you engage in banter with one person, another one may be listening and may approach. You should not shoo the person away just because you have come up with a plan with the first person. The movement to include more people may work in your favor.

The conversation below may be familiar to you, but with a slight twist.

You: What is your name?

Improv Partner: Stacey Stevens from HR.

You: Aha, Stacey Stevens from HR. Now, I know who to go to when I want to complain about Bob (make sure Bob is your friend) who has been badgering me with his Tik-Tok videos.

Improv Partner: Yes, you can go to me, or Bob can just show me his Tik-Tok videos.

Add in Bob (from a few feet away): My Tik-Tok videos are award-winning, Stacey!

You: Where are you from?

Improv Partner: I like saying I am from New York, but I actually have to commute from New Jersey early in the morning.

You: Wow! I don't know if I would be able to do that. So, I am just lying down on the floor of Bob's apartment until I can afford my own place.

Improv Partner: I am pretty sure you are kidding!

Add in Bob (getting a little closer): I've offered to share my bed, but he refuses (slight innuendo; keep it mild).

You: I am not. Who do you live with, by the way? Is it someone who snores like Bob? (Make sure Bob can hear this; wiggle your eyebrows at him to show him you are kidding.)

Add in Bob (very close now, a few inches from your face), just watching you intently. However, he is kidding.

Improv Partner: I bet I can beat you there. I live with my whole family: mom, dad, brother, sister, and sister's friend, who just would not leave the house. We are a rowdy bunch. I am pretty sure you have a much better time at Bob's.

Whatever movement you decide to use, it should keep on making you and your improv partner explore and discover various possible pathways for your conversation.

How do you make sure you create quality entertainment?

Let us inspect that word again: entertainment.

You must remember that you are not simply making conversation with another guest at a party: you are supposed to be the life of the party! Okay, perhaps that is pushing it a little bit. That also sounds a little arrogant. But hey, remember that your goal is to make people laugh.

Since you want to make people laugh, you have to shine the spotlight on yourself somehow. It does not have to be in a party setting. You could be at the office during lunchtime, trying to cheer up some of your officemates. You have noticed how they seem drained of energy, and there are still hours before home time.

You have to make someone laugh or at least smile. Because you have chosen to read this book, you have committed to being the source of entertainment.

So, the improv world that you are trying to build must have the hallmarks of good entertainment.

1. Where is the setting of your story? You cannot just fill the void of an empty room with grey walls. Describe its appearance, from its purpose to the actual décor. It may be a spaceship about to take off or a crowded restaurant.
2. Who are you in this skit? Are you an everyman? If so, then you have to make the most of that. Help that character connect with everyone else. More likely, they can relate to you. However, perhaps you can better entertain as a bald guy who lives across the street—you know, the one who always wears a fedora hat that keeps on flying off?

What should you do if the conversation does not go the way it is planned?

Well, this is improv, after all. Anything can happen. Just like life, your reaction to it is what makes or breaks the joke.

You are supposed to try to make people laugh. The emphasis is on the word "laugh." Of course, there is the possibility of failing in some sections of your joke. However, that does not mean to say that you just throw in the towel. You can continue pursuing the narrative if the only problem is getting the story to work as you envision it. When the material is the only issue, the other person can still be let in on the joke if you manage to meet him halfway.

Unfortunately, it is also possible that you have read a person wrong. Perhaps the other person is not interested in being part of your improv work. If a person wants out of the supposedly entertaining banter, let him go. You are not a standup comedian. The other person is not a fan who bought tickets to see a standup comedian. So, he may have other things to do, is too shy, or is just not interested in banter of any kind.

Do not take it seriously.

You are trying to entertain people. If it is stressing you out, it is just not worth it. You need your positivity and charm to stay strong.

It can be challenging to stay humorous if the subject itself is serious. Say, for example, you started talking to a colleague in the hopes of starting an improvised banter. Then, you are the one who got unpleasantly surprised because your intro has become a means for the other person to share what is wrong with him.

You: How was your weekend?

Other person: It was terrible. I slipped and fell right in front of my crush.

You: Oh, I am so sorry to hear that. Are you okay now?

Compare this to the following:

You: How was your weekend?

Other person: It was terrible. I slipped and fell right in front of my crush.

You: I always knew you were so smooth.

Other person: Yes, I slid right through the marble floor right next to his feet.

The first one shows how concerned you are for the other person. This reaction is, of course, socially acceptable. However, it does not make for a fun conversation. After you have raised your concern, the chance for improv laughs has already passed you by. You can only either keep quiet, move on to the next person, or just chat with this other person quietly. You may wait for a little bit more to take another chance at making her laugh.

The second instance allows you not to take the situation too seriously. Instead, you teased the other person by making a joke about her possibly embarrassing experience. This response lightens the mood for her, as well. So, you have made her laugh—or smile—and thus, you have helped her get over the situation.

Of course, not all situations are easy to joke about. You may want to get into a humorous banter about death, for example. Morbid jokes may only work if the case is not based on reality. For example, you may joke about the deaths or kills in a horror movie to make you feel less nervous about it.

Why should you go for the road less traveled?

When you plan improvised conversations, you don't want to stick to generic topics. Just how far can you go when you are talking about the weather, about your current status, and the like?

You need to spark your audience's interest. Start talking about more controversial topics, while keeping the conversation clean.

That should be a challenge.

Some comedians will urge you to use the "big guns": taboo topics, such as sex, religion, politics, family, and more. Well, you can joke about your family, but make sure you don't offend the family member, especially if you are joking around at home.

Politics and religion can place you in the line of fire. If you do not know the other person well, you may not know what their beliefs are. Instead of making someone laugh that day, you may end up creating a new foe. So, tread carefully. Do you want to get stressed that day? Nobody is paying you to make people laugh. It is just a genuine desire coming from you that makes you want to do that. If that will be rewarded with conflict, then you know that it is not worth it.

How do you think on your feet?

Improvisation comics must have enough wit and smarts to carry them through. Once you have put yourself on their feet, you will better appreciate the quick mental processes that whizz by in their heads to make the success of a joke possible.

It can be difficult, especially for a beginner.

But it is not impossible to learn.

How do you help yourself think on your feet better?

- You have to practice conversing with various people in your circles.
- Be genuinely concerned about how they are and what they can share with you.
- Be as knowledgeable as possible about topics that may interest your target.
- Practice on your own. Pick a random topic by flipping through the dictionary randomly or by preparing some strips of paper with subject matters and picking one of them. Then, just talk aloud about the topic like in an impromptu speech competition.

It is possible to get backed into a corner, especially when you are just starting. Here are a few things that you can do:

- Play word association games. When you hear a word but you don't exactly have a response to the particular context it was placed in, you can go another possible route. You can take that word in a more familiar direction.
- You can repeat the question that your target person asked you. This tactic will give you time to think of a witty answer. Reiterate it in such a way that you seem surprised that it was ever asked. Make a funny face as if you are bewildered that you have ever been asked that question. You have just made use of a pageant-style delaying tactic.
- You can express what you are feeling. Do so in an exaggerated manner. For example: "I am so sorry if I am not paying attention 100%. I am so tired!" Make a big show of yawning and stretching. This tactic may make it more slapstick material, but it can help you make the other person smile even when you may have run out of content for the time being.
- Ask a question. Maybe even turn the question to the person who asked it in the first place. It will surprise the

other person. Make it playful and not rude.

- Did you like the book that I wrote?
- Did I like the book that you wrote? What kind of question is that? Of course, I did. I still sleep with that book under my pillow. That is how much I like it. I am close to marrying it.

Thinking on your feet is better said than done. Thinking of the best retorts is sometimes better during the training stage. When you are in the middle of the conversation, it is possible to go blank. However, if you have entered the discussion with an open attitude and without taking yourself seriously, you should find a way to respond to anything wittily. Keep on practicing with a close friend who does not mind being a drill partner.

What is the importance of a callback in improv?

An improv can start simple enough. You plant the seeds carefully. You have to establish some "facts" in the world that you are about to build.

- A callback does not have to be laugh-out-loud funny. Sometimes, it is a groan-worthy moment. However, recalling it makes people laugh.
- A callback cannot be done right after the "facts" have been established. It is one of those moments wherein waiting is worth it.

An example of a callback in movies is a scene in *Airplane*! The cab driver leaves a passenger behind, saying he will just be back in a moment. However, the driver ends up boarding a plane and leaving. After a few minutes, the audience is assumed to have forgotten about the situation. The camera then goes back to the passenger. He is still in the cab. Seeing how ridiculous it is that this passenger decides to wait that long elicits laughter from the audience.

Using callback is very tricky, however. You can quickly alienate your audience members, especially if they were not paying attention. However, if you are sure that your audience was in it when you were establishing the scene, it might be worth exploring. Once you manage to pull off the callback and you get a knowing burst of laughter, then it is worth revisiting the same joke at a later date. The callback has become an inside joke.

Why do you need to let people talk?

Improv comedy or banter only works when you let other people talk as well. You cannot be hogging everything. People will be less inclined to speak to you if they notice that you don't listen.

Let others talk. This improv setup is not an official comedy partnership, but it can spell out your relationship in the future. While you may want to make your friends or colleagues laugh, they may also want to showcase their humor. You never know: your sense of humor may be compatible with others to the point that your future conversations will be more seamless and relaxed.

Talking too much can also be a sign of selfishness and disrespect. It is selfish because you are not allowing the other person to share their thoughts. It is disrespectful because you are cutting off their side of the communication. Yes, you may be the funniest among the group. Yes, you may be the one with the most material. However, it does not mean that you can dominate each conversation that you become a part of.

Silence also wields some power. Sometimes, it helps you with your comedic timing. It also allows you to be more open to what the other person has to say. The most effective funny responses originate from being able to listen to the other person carefully, instead of constantly thinking of the next thing to say. Yes, you can prepare the general setup. The details and flow, however, may have to depend on how the conversation ends up flowing.

The key to great improv comedy (or any type of conversation) is collaboration.

How would you fix this?

George: You look tired.

Fred: Yes, I am. I had a long night last night.

George: Oh, you know what? I have a trick to show you.

While it is true that Fred responds in a way that George does not find funny, it should not mean that he should just discard Fred's answer. George probably did not find any suitable material from the response and chose to move on. Do you think Fred is in any mood to laugh at any trick or joke George has in store for him? It does not seem that way. George had a clue all along: Fred is tired and may not be completely receptive. Also, he could have responded to Fred's current state. Then maybe Fred would have been more thankful and, therefore, more responsive.

This conversation could have happened:

George: You look tired.

Fred: Yes, I am. I had a long night last night.

George: I am sorry to hear that. Did you paint the town red again last night? (Fred is a homebody.)

Fred: (laughs) No. It is the same old thing. Work.

George: If you are going to tire yourself all night anyway, leave some time for fun. You are starting to look like my dad. (They are the same age.)

Fred: I might need to lighten up.

George: Oh, you know what? I have a trick to show you.

Framed better, both Fred and George get to say what they need to say.

How does "history" have to do with improv comedy?

No, we are not talking about textbook history here. We are referring to history in terms of what happened to you. Some characters call out history very well, like Sophia from the *Golden Girls*. When an event or topic reminds her of the past, she will start with:

"Sicily [insert year here],…."

When your friend and colleague talks about something that you cannot directly respond to, you can call out one of the topics or subtopics mentioned and relate it to an event that happened to you before.

Even in a non-comedic situation, it can work.

Friend: I lost my wallet in the worst place possible! I lost it right in the mall.

[You have several possible paths here: losing your wallet, doing something at the worst place possible, losing something at the mall, the last time you were at the mall, etc.]

You (response 1): Are you kidding? I just lost my wallet last week, but it was at the cafeteria. I was already picturing how it would unfold, but someone had found it and gave it to me. I was so thankful I did not ask about why there was a missing $20 bill from it."

You (response 2): It reminds me that I cursed in the worst place possible last Sunday—at church. Fr. Luke was right behind me. He was pretending he didn't hear. Was it a sin for priests to pretend anything?

You (response 3): I just lost something at the mall the other day—well, thankfully, it was only for a moment. It was my son.

You (response 4): I cannot remember when I was last at the mall. It is a dangerous place.

So, you can see that by simply digging up through your history, you can find some possibly serious answers and wisecracks, too.

How do you use exaggerated similes and metaphors to your advantage?

Ever since you were a child, you have been taught what a metaphor is. You know that you are comparing two different things without using "like a" or "as ____as a." In that way, it differs from a simile.

Some similes have been overused:

- As bright as the sun
- As cold as ice

Some metaphors have also been overused:

- Drinking the Kool-Aid
- Laughingstock
- Deadline
- In the same boat
- Green with envy

Then, some similes have their serious beginnings, but have been subjected to parody:

- "Life is like a box of chocolates; you never know what you're gonna get."
    - Life is like a box of chocolates; halfway through, you realize how much you hate yourself. (One of the clean parody versions you can find online.)

With improv jokes, however, sometimes you can go all the way crazy with your metaphors and similes.

Here are some possible zany descriptions:

- Going shopping with Zelma is like going to war because you have to weaponize yourself with either a credit card or a blind eye to all that she says is good for you.

- Whenever you visit Alfred, make sure your stomach is empty. You cannot say no to his wife's cooking, and she cooks up quite a storm when she knows Alfred's friends are coming over.
- I like how cupcakes taste like the end of my dreams of joining a beauty pageant in this lifetime. Then, I remember that I am also too short and too opinionated to be accepted or to go through all the grinning and waving.

The wordiness is part of the exaggerated response or statement. You may start with 0 and end up with a 100. I know. The term "from zero to hero" popped into your head, but I am trying to avoid it just like a child's gaze avoiding his mother's after she opened his report card and found all the red marks all over it.

Other descriptions that may not fall under similes and metaphors, but still create a particular "so vivid, it's so funny feel."

1. Oh, you are asking what type of mom I am? Sorry, I am not a soccer mom. That is too generic. I am a watch-like-a-hawk while working both full time and part time, tiger slash soccer mom.
2. At the office, I am the "eat fast while standing at the pantry and gulp my drink so that I can avoid other people" type of employee.

How do you use exaggerated reactions to your advantage?

So, you have already done quite your share with exaggeration, using similes and metaphors. Now, you are going to try performing exaggeration expressions and reactions. George Peart's "You Can Be Funny & Make People Laugh" refers to this as the YouTuber's reaction. He is right. There is something in that.

Have you watched YouTube videos? More likely, you have. Some people are addicted to these videos and have even subscribed to some channels. Usually, the channels that rise to popularity are those that can lighten up and be funny if they cannot deliver the celebrity status.

When I am talking about YouTuber reactions, however, I am talking about those that do unboxing videos. These YouTubers would not normally open boxes like children, but for their videos, they seem to go back in time: eyes wide, mouth open, and voices full of wonder. You may either get amused or annoyed by such a display. However, if a friend of yours does this little stunt offline, you may burst out laughing. You cannot believe that your friend can be this amazed by, say, a new pen.

Yes, the humbler the object of your awe, the funnier it will be. There is some acting involved here in most cases. To make it work better, though, you can start with objects that you are genuinely in awe of that your friends just do not understand.

What about making up a story as you go along?

Remember when you were a kid at school? Your teacher has suddenly decided it is time to patch a story together. She will start with one sentence. Then, the next child will add something to that story, and the rest of the class will add to it, and so forth.

If you were a bubbly kid, then this would have been your chance to shine. Bubbliness would not have been enough, though. You also needed to think on your feet, which is basically what most of improv is all about.

Conversely, if you were a shy kid with a quick mind, then all the magic would have been happening in your head. Yes, you may start giggling quietly, but you just made yourself laugh. Other people in your class had no idea what you were thinking about.

Today, the bubbly kid with fewer ideas would have to open himself to the process. If you were this kid, then you already have the personality to carry the conversation. Do not overthink. Stories can start as serious but can be buoyed by someone else in the group. Similarly, stories can become hilarious without you trying. Again, it is all in how much you practice.

On the other hand, the shy kid with ideas would just have to go with it. Do not let those ideas die down without anyone hearing about them. Share!

Coming up with a funny story should have been taught in school at some point. At that time, it falls under the generic category of writing a story, any story. So, you just have to be creative but in a fun way.

Stories begin with prompts such as:

- What if this happens?
- A character goes to this place because he wants to achieve his goal but encounters problems along the way.

You can begin with a simple "what if" question.

- What if I wake up tomorrow to discover that giant poodles have taken over the city?
- What if my boss decides to give us truckloads of pizza instead of our cash salary?
- What if my friend decides he cannot stand me because I wear blue shirts all the time?

These storytelling prompts may in themselves be funny or ridiculous, depending on what you can come up with.

Exercise:

Can you give at least three "What if" statements that you can use in real life?

Another variation of the above exercise is to create hypothetical scenarios such as the following:

- The family eating at the next table look intent in munching their lettuce. They all look like calorie counters.
- I don't think I should stay on this planet anymore. Look at how human beings treat me. Even dogs bark at me as if I look like a thief.

Exercise:

Use the prompts below to make up your own jokes:

1. You are trapped in a spaceship, with nothing else but the suit you have on and a violin.
____
____
____
____
____

2. It was still dark when you woke up. You did not hear your alarm, but you are wide awake.
____
____
____
____
____

3. Your grandma turns 103 tomorrow. She wants you to be there at 7 o'clock sharp.

____
____
____
____

4. A neighbor has been screaming wildly for a few minutes now. You cannot rush to her because

____
____
____
____

5. A dog approaches you, sniffing your shoes.

____
____
____
____

You can play scenarios like these at a party or get-together. It is like a recreation of the classroom game from when you were little. The more creative and outlandish the details become, the more hilarious it can be.

You know your team better. The personalities and preferences of your friends and colleagues will ultimately decide the details that can be added. Let it be clear that off-color, offensive, and highly sexualized jokes should not be added to the brew.

What about imagining the consequences of an event or action?

Sometimes, people's assumptions can be hurtful, annoying, and offensive. We have dealt with such assumptions throughout our lives. Sadly, we also make the same types of assumptions about other people.

What if the consequences are pretty much a given among a group of friends or family members? Then, it becomes inside information. Inside information can be converted to inside jokes, depending on how you treat the information. It is in how you treat the facts given, rather than the facts themselves. We have mentioned this earlier in the book. Some people always find humor in even the most disastrous events. However, finding humor in cases such as death can be offensive any which way you look at it.

Read the following situations and observe how they make their predictions or assumptions humorous:

- Stacey: Eva is going to join a pageant.

  Lisa: Wow! She would win it if she did not end up tripping on her heels and falling on the judges.

  (Stacey and Lisa BOTH KNOW how pretty Eva is, but they also BOTH KNOW that Eva is clumsy and is probably not comfortable wearing heels. So, they ASSUME that there is a possibility that she may fall on heels.)

  Using someone as the object of a joke is a little cruel. The situation can only be mitigated if Eva is friends with the two, and she is also aware of her inherent awkwardness.

  An inoffensive, but slightly dull version of the above would be:

  Stacey: Eva is going to join a pageant.

  Lisa: Wow! She is pretty enough to win, but she needs to practice on heels. She can be quite clumsy.

- John: Let us go to Lulu's place.

  Tony: Oh, you want me to go with you? You just want someone who can guide you through that maze of a neighborhood.

  (John and Tony have been to Lulu's place. It seems that John has no sense of direction, and Lulu's house is in a neighborhood with lots of twists and turns. As the third wheel, Tony feels like he has only been asked because of one particular reason.)

Tony could well just say "Yes" to the invitation, staying polite and loyal to his friend, John. He may also just say "No" because he knows what his role would have been like. However, Tony has decided to show John that he is fully aware of the situation, but he is still willing to help. It may sound like a rough answer, but Tony is still down for the ride.

How do you add in crazy explanations?

Formal and factual responses are helpful. They are informative. But are they funny? Most of the time, they are not. There is a possibility that a fact can still be entertaining, but you may not always get that chance.

Here are some conversations with crazy explanations:

- Ted: Andy got 100% on the exam. There is no way he could have cheated with the way Mr. Phillip was watching all of us.

Luis: His parents did not see him at dinner last night. He might have been abducted by aliens and returned with a full computer chip in his head before anybody noticed.

This conversation could have gone entirely factual, like:

Ted: Andy got 100% on the exam. There is no way he could have cheated with the way Mr. Phillip was watching all of us.

Luis: His parents did not see him at dinner last night. He might have studied from the afternoon until night at the library.

Luis could have utilized the second response, but he would instead put in a highly creative, funny reply. There is an assumption here that both boys do not believe Andy would get high marks unless he had supernatural or extraordinary help.

- Farrah (the babysitter): Mr. and Mrs. Fielding, I am going home! Danny has been so well-behaved today. I got scared for a minute and thought he was sick.

Mr. Fielding: Danny was well-behaved. Well, honey (turns to his wife), the Diazepam that we gave him worked out quite well!

Of course, the above is merely a joke. However, it could have gone this way:

Farrah (the babysitter): Mr. and Mrs. Fielding, I am going home! Danny has been so well-behaved today. I got scared for a minute and thought he was sick.

Mr. Fielding: Danny was well-behaved. Well, honey (turns to his wife), I gave him the talk last night. Danny has been very receptive.

Again, factual responses are helpful but are rarely funny. You may want to switch to humorous answers from time to time, depending on the mood that you plan to create.

How do you let the other person fill in the blanks?

How another person fills in the blanks for you can result in hilarious misunderstandings or funny but accurate conclusions.

Take a look at this conversation:

Amber: Are you going to join us at the concert tomorrow?

Taylor: My mom will visit me at my dorm.

Amber: Uh, oh.

Taylor does not directly respond to Amber's question. However, an understanding passes from one girl to the other. An observer may not know what is up. Here is possible missing information:

- Taylor's mom is very strict. She will not allow Taylor to attend the concert.
- Taylor's mom is too fun-loving. She might want to get invited to the concert, as well.
- Taylor's boyfriend is staying in the dorm. She would be in trouble with her mom, thus endangering her concert plans.

When some information is omitted, we can assume that both persons talking should have the extra information tucked in somewhere.

If you leave out information on purpose, make sure you do it with someone who knows you or your situation well. This tactic can be hilarious as an improv skit because you can make the other members of the audience raise their eyebrows in suspicion or recognition.

The above examples are a testament that improv conversations and jokes cannot be planned. However, you need to do the following:

- Be receptive. Listen to the other person well.
- Be in good humor. If you have a positive outlook, then you are more likely to engage in fun banter.
- Keep away from possibly offensive humor.
- Have a good knowledge of the other person's sense of humor or at least overall personality.

Not everyone will want to be part of your extended banter. Short quips may establish your desire to communicate in this fun manner. Someone will likely take the bait within your circle of friends or colleagues. According to the *Psychological Science* article, "The

Science of Humor is no Laughing Matter," people are more likely to laugh at videos with canned laughter. Now, you are not in a video. You are also not a professional comedian. However, if you can find people who can respond to you—like some kind of clique—you may be able to recreate that effect in real life. Perhaps, you can do it as a duo kind of natural performance.

Part Eight – Going Back Inwards

"My life has been one great big joke, a dance that's walked a song that's spoke. I laugh so hard I almost choke when I think about myself." - Maya Angelou

Whenever you feel like you are lost in your improv game or even just your witty, conversational skills, you have to go back to yourself.

One thing that you will never forget is yourself. As long as you remain honest with yourself and others, you have a self that you can go back to. You don't have to be dishonest to be funny. You can take the truth and look at it at a humorous angle.

No matter how truthful you are, however, you still have to follow some rules:

1. You cannot take everything seriously and literally.
2. You must be ready to laugh at yourself.
3. You need to put as much energy and enthusiasm as possible into the situation.

The above are just some of the unspoken rules.

Well, if you take things at face value all the time, you sound boring. You are one of those people in novels who "say" and "reply" and "speak" or whatever other non-enthusiastic verbs the author can attach to you.

You are just there, saying facts.

Facts are excellent; that is a given. However, you are trying to make people laugh. You are not a reporter narrating the news. You are also not a scientist explaining graphs and charts that other people could not understand.

You have to take something—a fact—and twirl it around in your head and spin it further with your words until everyone is heady with laughter.

So, your friend tells you that it was too cold outside. How do you respond?

Concerned, but very literal and boring: Oh, did you at least have your coat on?

Affirms the statement, but still very literal and boring: Yes, I was just outside. I had to clutch at my coat tighter.

Well, some of us indeed have a powerful motherly or fatherly inclination to care for others. So, this response comes from within you. It is genuine, as well, and should not be discarded; it is part of who you are.

However, you consulted this book for a reason. You want to make people laugh. Then, you have to find material within yourself that you will want to laugh about, as well.

Will the following responses fare better?

Flirty, but joking: At least you are here now. Just sit close to me. I have enough heat to warm you up. (Make sure that this is only done with close friends. You don't want to be sued for sexual harassment. You can even be self-deprecatory in the end, to show that the response usually is not the type you go for.)

Referencing a movie: But I thought the cold never bothered you, anyway. (This is safer but will have to rely on a callback. The other person should either have said that he/she did not mind the cold or have clearly stated that he/she is a fan of *Frozen*, the animated movie.)

Referring to the current situation: Are you complaining now? The office a/c usually freezes us over every day, anyway. That's why I made sure I have at least five different sweaters to settle in comfortably and fashionably.

Going for an inside joke or inside knowledge: Oh, you're feeling cold now? Wait until Mrs. Thomas comes. I heard she was raised in the wilds of Siberia. She sweats in this kind of temperature.

Exercise

Respond to the following questions and statements in two ways: formal and humorous:

1. What is the latest news about the storm?
2. Who will wash the dishes tonight?
3. Where do you think we should bring your dad for his birthday?
4. Why are you still sleeping at 10 am?
5. When is your anniversary?

We just used the five Ws to create some possible scenarios.

Formal responses :

1. The storm has strengthened further. The news reporter said we would start feeling it by tomorrow night.
2. I believe it is Caitlyn's turn. I washed the dishes last night.
3. Dad likes burgers. I know it is not good for him, but since it is his birthday, we can bring him to that new burger place across the pharmacy.
4. Sorry, I was so tired last night. I had to finish a report for work. Then, when I was done, I had problems sleeping.
5. My anniversary isn't until next week.

Formal responses have to stick to the facts. You cannot do much about it. You may try becoming more literary about it, but you cannot really change the details.

Possible humorous responses:

1. Do you know what the name of the storm is? Yeah, it has the same name as our delivery guy. So, while the weather

station says it should be here at 11 pm tomorrow night, you may have to wait a few more hours later.

(This joke will work if the person you are talking to knows the guy you are talking about.)

2. For sure, it is not going to be me for a few more nights. I washed a gazillion dishes last night because of Caitlyn's party. She has a few more nights' duty to pay for it since she did not help at all last night.

(The delivery is crucial here. This can easily sound more petty than funny.)
It could be simpler, like:
Oh, I know it is not going to be my turn for a few more nights, right, Caitlyn?
(This can be done in a teasing way.)

3. Dad will gladly go anywhere with food, booze, and an agreeable version of mom.

(While this may have a playful delivery, it can also reveal some truths about the marriage. Dad seems to be happy if he has his favorite things. He has simple wishes.)

4. Why was I still sleeping at 10 am? What were you doing sending me messages at 5 am? Are you the sun? Everyone else I know was snoring when you were texting me.

(Notice that the response started by repeating the question asked. This is the person biding his time. He was able to ask the other person a question, as well. This response suggests that it was not him who was strange by sleeping in at 10 am, but his friend who was awake as early as 5 am.)

The friend can rebut this, as well, to continue the banter:

*Excuse me. Wasn't it you who said we were going jogging early this morning? You would rather work on your report late at night than wake up to make sure you can still work years from now.

5. If I don't get my wife something she likes, there may as well be no anniversary—again.

(This response suggests that he does not get to celebrate his wedding anniversary the way he expects to do so whenever he cannot please his wife. There should be a short pause after "anniversary," wait for the reaction, then reveal that it has happened before.)

Comedic Persona

Part of going back to yourself is analyzing whether you were able to create a comedic persona. You have reached this far, but perhaps you are still struggling with your implementation.

If you have failed in some way, remind yourself: you are not a comedian. You are a person who only wants to make other people laugh, and that is an admirable trait. Failing from time to time should be part of the agenda. With failures, you can learn more. You will realize, "Oh, that did not work out because I was so busy focusing on my script and not my audience." It may also be a case of the joke not really aligning with your personality.

According to the book, *How to Kill in Comedy,* a comedic persona is made up of four parts: Flaw, BlindSpot, Attitude, and Agenda.

Most of your favorite comedians filled in the four parts of a comedic persona, whether they know it or not. If you can create a structure for your comedic persona, your jokes may become more consistent, purposeful, and yet also authentic to who you are.

So, let us explore one of the comedic personas that were discussed in the same book referenced above—Jim Carrey. He is an identifiable comedian. So, we are going to look at his flaw, blindspot, attitude, and agenda.

According to *How to Kill in Comedy,* Jim Carry has Attention Deficit Disorder. Some of us may agree, and some of us may consider him as a childish, super hyper, almost lunatic type. His blind spot is that he is not aware of the vibe that he gives off. His attitude shows his real self. So, his agenda is to make people believe that he can behave normally and rationally.

If you have been watching his movies, you will notice that he usually follows these four parts. The movie version of *A Series of Unfortunate Events* was able to showcase his ability through a character that was close to his comedic persona. Count Olaf is always running around pretending to be a different, saner character, but he is ultimately a crazy, self-absorbed villain. Jim Carry has had other similar stints such as *Dumb and Dumber*, *Ace Ventura: Pet Detective*, *Liar, Liar*, and more.

Now, let us take a look at you.

Perhaps the reason some of your jokes work more than others is that your comedic persona is either non-existent or inconsistent. The jokes that may have worked may have been closer to who you are as a person. So, you were able to incorporate them into a conversation without a lot of issues.

Here is a possible comedic persona: the Tiger-Soccer Mom

Flaw: possessive, obsessive

Blindspot: her determination to raise her kids the ways she likes

Attitude: pretends to be relaxed and casual, but obviously gritting her teeth when trying to make small talk

Agenda: Raise A+ students who are good at sports and just about everything, without making it look like a struggle—which it is

You don't have to be a tiger-soccer mom in real life. However, you need to have some of the main ingredients: achievers for kids, a seemingly tough look, and a deadpan delivery. It will help if you are joking around with people who know the real you: a mom who is serious about her kids' achievements but not to the point of obsession. You just exaggerated your authentic self. So, it was not hard to get into character. This character can randomly pop up during discussions about related topics: children, achievements, sports, and anything else that you can associate with the comedic persona.

Another comedic persona: Kindhearted buddy who pretends to be tough

Flaw: Big guy, but really a fraidy cat

Blindspot: Thinks people do not know that he quickly gets scared

Attitude: Pretends to be tough and gruff, even going as far as making his voice deeper

Agenda: Appear to assist and save people when he is more scared than them

This comedic persona will work if you are a big guy, not necessarily a scaredy-cat but someone willing to play the role.

Part Nine - More Jokes

"Everyone has a sense of humor. If you don't laugh at jokes, you probably laugh at opinions."
— Criss Jami, Killosophy

As we wind down to the end of this ebook, we will take a look at a few more joke styles that you can try to incorporate into your conversations. We have made use of several self-deprecating jokes and jokes that appeal to your sense of humor. Most professional comedians do the same thing, apparently. They look at their own lives and come up with a wealth of material. The way that they joke about these aspects of their lives shows that they don't really look down at themselves, as the words may suggest.

1. Exaggeration Formula

The idea of using exaggeration to make anything funny has been mentioned before. However, a formula may help to drive this concept in using only one or two lines.

Example:
I drink **too** much **that** the bar had to close down hours before midnight.
The keywords here are "too" and "that." Can you think of a sentence that will make use of this simple exaggeration formula?

2. Too Much Information

Sometimes, TMI jokes still skirt closely to the self-deprecating jokes. However, sometimes, they are just there to make the other person either uncomfortable, laughing hard, or both. This is best delivered deadpan to counter the possibly shocking detail.

Example:
Setup: I love Saturdays.
Ordinary related information about the setup:
These are the days when you could probably lounge on the couch, don't shower until the afternoon…

TMI: Or realize that you need to do extra work because your girlfriend asked you to pay for her credit card bills. Since she is so smart and pretty, all you could do is say "yes" to all the work and preparing her dinner for that same Saturday night.
Back to normal: Yeah, Saturdays are heavenly.

3. Crazy Facts

Sometimes, going back to your own crazy life may just be the trick to make your friends or colleagues laugh, scoff, or watch you with bewilderment. Your delivery will have to win the game for this one.

Here are some possible crazy facts:

- When I was nine, I read *The Exorcist.* Nobody really minded me much because they were too focused on my constantly-high cousin throwing stones at the local clinic. It was also probably a time when people were still flexible about parental guidance and such.
- My music teacher had this habit of letting us sing in front of the blackboard so that we would not feel too shy. I felt even more ridiculous.
- My brother used to like catching lizards and moths. He would experiment with them with water in a pot.

For some people, crazy facts themselves can make them laugh or at least see in a new, albeit strange, light. For others, you may want to add fictional details to drive the humor home. The above can work with the follow-ups below:

- When I was ten, and everyone had relaxed, I could not even score a Stephen King paperback, and they started looking at my Nancy Drews suspiciously.
- Now, whenever I feel shy about something, I still have the tendency to turn around and look for a blackboard to talk to.
- I am just glad that he is now a surgeon, not a serial killer. Or should I be happy?

4. Knock-Knock Jokes

Oh, they do still work with some people. If you cannot get a laugh, then you can at least get a groan with a smile. Nobody can really blame you for trying to make people laugh unless you are making it obnoxious and in-your-face.

There is an extensive collection of jokes out there for you to use. You can get silly and corny sometimes, but do not forget to avoid tasteless jokes that rely on sexuality, putting others down, stereotyping, and offensiveness. It is better to take yourself as an example rather than pick on someone else. After all, your goal is to make people laugh. You want them to laugh hilariously, giggle, smile, or even groan from time to time. You are not out there to reduce them to tears, anger, or defensiveness. The joke styles that you have learned from this book are meant for fun and sharing great times together.

Conclusion

Have you tried any of the strategies and joke types that are included in this book? How was it? Did it work right away, or did you have to warm up and wait for people to get connected with your joke style?

You will find that it is better to practice with family members and close friends. They are more likely to tell you if your jokes are funny or corny. They will be brutally honest with their feedback. After all, they will be the ones who will likely be at the receiving end of your efforts.

Of course, even if they find your jokes funny, there will still be a chance that others will not. Don't be hard on yourself. More likely, people who will not laugh at your jokes are not receptive in the first place. If you start taking it personally, then it will be challenging for you to take things lightly and attempt again. We don't know what problems the other person is going through.

In real life, you can plan to make a joke, but you still need to be more spontaneous. The spontaneous jokes are the ones that usually work best. They work best because you are more relaxed and open to how the scene will unfold.

So, lighten up! This way, you can help others lighten up. Go out there and make people laugh. It is a noble cause and a beautiful contribution to this world.

Thank you!

Before you go, I just wanted to say thank you for purchasing my book.

You could have picked from dozens of other books on the same topic but you took a chance and chose this one.

So, a HUGE thanks to you for getting this book and for reading all the way to the end.

Now I wanted to ask you for a small favor. ***Could you please consider posting a review on the platform? Reviews are one of the easiest ways to support the work of independent authors.***

This feedback will help me continue to write the type of books that will help you get the results you want. So if you enjoyed it, please let me know! (-:

Resources Page

Andal, Elizabeth. "7 Reasons Why We Should All Develop Our Sense Of Humor." Lifehack, Lifehack, 3 Aug. 2015, www.lifehack.org/articles/lifestyle/7-scientific-reasons-why-should-laugh-more.html.

Cabane, O. F. (2013). The charisma myth: How anyone can master the art and science of personal magnetism. New York: Portfolio/Penguin.

Ciampa, Dan, and Various Authors. "When Charismatic Leadership Goes Too Far." Harvard Business Review, 6 Mar. 2017, hbr.org/2016/11/when-charismatic-leadership-goes-too-far.

Creativestandup.com, creativestandup.com/introvert-or-extrovert-in-stand-up-comedy/#:~:text=Comedians%20like%20Steve%20Martin%2C%20Woody,%2Dproclaimed%20introverts%20in%20entertainment).

Dean EskichFollowidea machine, et al. "The 4 Types Of Charisma And How You Can Use Them." LinkedIn, www.linkedin.com/pulse/20140707152439-208261461-the-4-types-of-charisma-and-how-you-can-use-them/.

King, Patrick. Improv(e) Your Conversations: Think on Your Feet, Witty Banter, and Always Know What to Say with Improv Comedy Techniques. CreateSpace Independent Publishing Platform, 2017.

Markman, Art. "Humor Sometimes Makes Stressful Situations Better." Psychology Today, Sussex Publishers, 21 June 2017, www.psychologytoday.com/us/blog/ulterior-motives/201706/humor-sometimes-makes-stressful-situations-better.

MasterClass. "The 10 Most Popular Types of Jokes - 2020." MasterClass, MasterClass, 2 July 2019, www.masterclass.com/articles/the-10-most-popular-types-of-jokes#is-there-a-basis-for-every-joke.

Michel, Alexandra. "The Science of Humor Is No Laughing Matter." Association for Psychological Science - APS, 31 Mar. 2017, www.psychologicalscience.org/observer/the-science-of-humor-is-no-laughing-matter.

Oelze, Patricia. "Types Of Humor And What They Say About Your Personality." Betterhelp, BetterHelp, 15 Apr. 2018, www.betterhelp.com/advice/general/types-of-humor-and-what-they-say-about-your-personality/.

Peart, Geoffrey. You Can Be Funny and Make People Laugh: No Theories: No Fluff: 35 Humor Techniques That Work for Everyday Conversations. Aurelius Books, 2019.

Restauri, Denise. "5 Qualities of Charismatic People. How Many Do You Have?" Forbes, Forbes Magazine, 11 Sept. 2014, www.forbes.com/sites/deniserestauri/2012/05/03/5-qualities-of-charismatic-people-how-many-do-you-have/.

Robinson, Lawrence. "Laughter Is the Best Medicine." HelpGuide.org, www.helpguide.org/articles/mental-health/laughter-is-the-best-medicine.htm.

www.ingramcontent.com/pod-product-compliance
Lightning Source LLC
Chambersburg PA
CBHW081723250726
48657CB00010B/3098
9798340678386